Discovering Cool Japan

Akiko Tsuda   Kayoko Kinshi   Christopher Valvona

 **SEIBIDO**

photographs by
iStockphoto

StreamLine

Web 動画のストリーミング再生について

Web 動画マークがある箇所は、PC、スマートフォン、タブレット端末において、無料でストリーミング再生することができます。下記 URL よりご利用ください。再生手順や動作環境などは本書巻末の「Web 動画のご案内」をご覧ください。

http://st.seibido.co.jp

本書は、NHK-BS1 で 2016 年〜 2017 年に放送された「COOL JAPAN　発掘! かっこいいニッポン」の英語放送より、13 の番組の一部をもとに書籍化したものです。

Discovering Cool Japan

はじめに

　このテキストでは、NHK の人気番組、『COOL JAPAN　発掘! かっこいいニッポン』をもとに、日本人が当たり前と思ってきた日本の文化や技術が外国の人たちにはかっこいいモノとして受け入れられている 13 のテーマについて、ニッポンの魅力と秘密を探ります。外国人が実際に体験する日本文化の現地レポートと、様々な国の出演者が自国文化と日本文化の違いを語るスタジオディスカッションの 2 部構成の映像を見ながら、世界各国の多様な文化背景を持つスピーカーの考えに触れ、日本文化を再認識し、世界へ向けて英語で発信する力を養います。

　『COOL JAPAN』では、英語を第一言語とするアメリカやイギリス、オーストラリアなどの話者だけでなく、ヨーロッパ諸国やアジア、アフリカ、ラテンアメリカなど、各国のスピーカーが登場し、英語を共通語として（English as a Lingua Franca,　以下 ELF）駆使し、活発に議論します。英語を国際コミュニケーションの道具として使うことの重要性を考え、日本事象について自ら発信できることを目標に様々なタスクに挑戦してみましょう。それぞれのユニットの最後には、英語母語話者によるトピックに関連したリーディングを掲載していますので活用してください。

　なお、このテキストは番組をそのまま活用した Authentic な ELF 教材ですが、標準米語も一緒に学べるように、巻末に英語母語話者が書き起こしたスクリプトも掲載しています。本書によって皆さんが日本文化について再考し、世界各国のスピーカーの多様な英語に触れ、ELF に興味を持つきっかけづくりになれば幸いです。

　最後になりましたが、本書の作成にあたり、成美堂の田村栄一氏、佐野泰孝氏、佐野泰一氏には企画段階から大変お世話になりました。この場を借りて心からお礼を申し上げます。

津田晶子

金志佳代子

クリストファー・ヴァルヴォーナ

本書の構成と使い方

iv

 **PART 1 REPORT VIEWING**

ユニットで扱うテーマについて、海外からのスピーカーが各地に赴き、レポートします。日本人が当たり前と思ってきた文化や技術は、外国人レポーターの目からはどのように映るのか、日本文化の再認識や異文化理解の一助を担うパートとして視聴してみましょう。

✿ *Warm-up*

テーマに関する質問です。ペアまたはグループで考えてみましょう。

✿ *Vocabulary Building*

REPORT VIEWING で使用される5単語のマッチング問題です。授業でのニーズに応じて、REPORT VIEWING 視聴の前に学習しても効果的です。

PART 2 STUDIO DISCUSSION VIEWING

REPORT VIEWING に出演した外国人レポーターに加え、男女の司会者と各国のスピーカーが REPORT VIEWING の内容に沿って本音で活発に議論しています。テキストには異文化理解の助けとなるよう、各スピーカーの名前の下に国旗を掲載しています。各国のスピーカーの意見や価値観を捉え、日本文化を再認識する場として視聴してください。

✿ *T or F Questions*

映像を視聴して内容理解の確認をします。正誤問題に答えましょう。

✿ *Dictation*

リスニングの空所補充問題です。ペアやグループで協力して回答してもよいでしょう。米国のスピーカーが米国で一般的な文法や表現に則って、一部変更したスクリプトを巻末に「Listening (dubbed soundtrack)」として掲載しています。このスクリプトを基にして米国人が吹き替え直した音声は、Classroom DVD とストリーミング配信サービスにも収録していますので、授業のニーズに応じて活用してください。ストリーミング配信サービス（StreamLine）の使用方法は巻末を参照ください。

> What's your opinion?

> What do you think about it?

各スピーカーの意見について、自分の考えをまとめてみましょう。授業でのニーズに応じて、ディスカッションの設問として活用するのも良いでしょう。

Useful expressions

STUDIO DISCUSSION VIEWING で実際に使われている、英語のディスカッションにおける便利な表現を紹介します。本文では太文字（bold）にしています。

❋ Matching

4人のスピーカーの意見と写真のマッチング問題です。各スピーカーの意見を確認しましょう。

❋ Discussion

視聴した映像の内容を基にしたディスカッション用の設問です。ペア、またはグループで考えてみましょう。トピックの内容の定着をはかります。

❋ Presenting Japan to the World

日本文化を発信するための発展問題です。グループでプレゼンテーションをしてみましょう。

❋ Further Reading

ユニットの内容に関連したリーディングです。音読したり、シャドーイングしたりするのに適した文章です。

Write your own ideas

Further Reading を読んで自分の意見を書き出してみましょう。

CONTENTS

Long-Established Businesses

老舗

cool japan

日本は 100 年以上続く老舗が多いことで知られています。老舗のブランドはどうやって守り続けられてきたのか、外国人は日本の老舗をどう考えているのか、「日本の老舗の秘密」を探ってみましょう。

PART 1 REPORT VIEWING

David と Heike は、銀座にある老舗を見学に出かけています。日本の老舗にはどんな特色があるでしょうか。映像を見た後に、下記の質問に答えてみましょう。

✴ Warm-up

以下の質問に対して、ペアまたはグループで話し合ってみましょう。

1. Are there any businesses where you live that have existed for a long time? What kind of businesses are they?

2. Which would you like to work for: a long-established business or a new and promising business?

✴ Vocabulary Building

(a)–(e) に対応する英訳を (1)–(5) から選びましょう。

(a) 眼鏡店 （　　）	(b) 新生児 （　　）	(c) 許可 （　　）
(d) 調節 （　　）	(e) 任せる （　　）	

(1) newborn　　(2) optician　　(3) adjustment　　(4) entrust　　(5) permission

PART 2 STUDIO DISCUSSION VIEWING

✴ T or F Questions

映像の内容と一致する場合には T に、しない場合には F に○をつけましょう。

1. Australia is listed in the top 10 countries that have long-established businesses.　　　　T　　F

2. In Bulgaria, the number of long-established businesses declined due to political issues.　　　　T　　F

3. The U.S. businesses tend to focus on expanding globally.　　　　T　　F

Long-Established Businesses

✳ *Dictation*

映像を見て、空欄を埋めましょう。

Shoji Kokami:
(Male Presenter)
Well, what do you all think about this?

Joo Sunyi:
South Korea
Yeah, I think it's very nice, because in Korea there are very, very few long-established shops in Korea, so…

5

Male Presenter: OK. What do you think, Irina?

Irina Babanova:
Bulgaria
It was great, actually. They adapted their product and services to the need 10 of the customer.

Male Presenter: OK.

3

Craig Taylor:
Australia
Ah yeah, well it's, um, it's one of the main ways a business can stay in business — is by (^{1}) the customer. That's a really (^{2}) (^{3}). 15

Male Presenter: Yes.

Do you agree with Arne?

Arne van Lamoen:
Netherlands
I think this level of service is something that I miss back home. I think we used to have it, and we don't have it anymore. Japanese service is still so good, that I think it surprises people.

Male Presenter: Oh, really?

20

Risa Stegmayer:
(Female Presenter)
All right. Let's take a look at (^{4}) (^{5}) long-established businesses Japan actually has. The board, please. Looking at the number of businesses (^{6}) more than 100 years, by country, this one, Japan comes first with 25,321 businesses.

Male Presenter: Wow. 25

Female Presenter: Yes, it is a first by a (⁷   ) margin. (⁸   ) (⁹   )
(¹⁰   ) as many as the U.S. in second place.

Male Presenter: Amazing.

Why do you think it is?

Female Presenter: Looking at the other countries, after the U.S. come many European
countries. By the way, Craig's Australia is in 11th place, with 709 30
businesses. And Brazil, Bulgaria, and Sunyi's South Korea don't even
make it into the top 20. What distinguishes long-established Japanese
businesses is that many are small-scale family businesses. **In contrast, in
the U.S., it is large long-established businesses that stand out.**

4

What's your opinion?

Male Presenter: I see. Do you think it's cool that there are many long-established 35
businesses, or is this not cool?

Arne: Yeah, I think it's
cool, but I think it's
amazing.

Male Presenter: Really? Who thinks 40
this is cool? Really?

Craig: Of course.

Male Presenter: It's cool? How about
long-established businesses in your countries? What's different?

David Pavlina: Well, in the U.S….the U.S. is a very young country, (¹¹   ) 45
U.S.
(¹²   ) Japan, so our very oldest business would just be from
the late 1700s. Also, the, the most famous are very global, international

corporations. I also think that they appeal to the American sense of patriotism. I always imagine long-established businesses are things like riding a Harley, wearing blue jeans, drinking Coca-Cola, and playing a Gibson guitar or something like that.

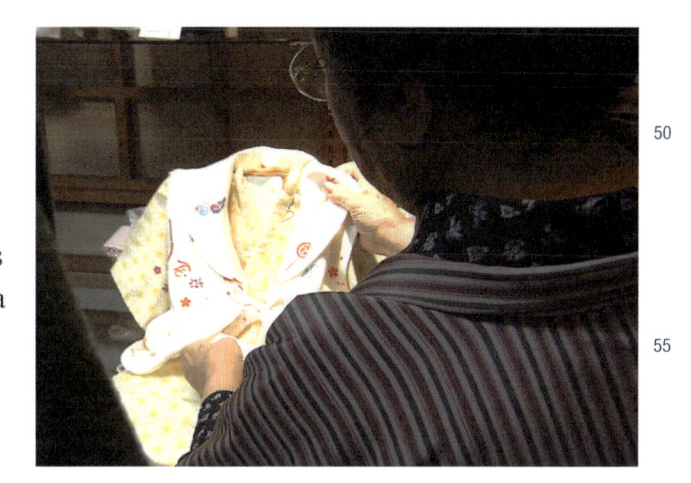

50

55

Male Presenter: I see. Well what about the Netherlands?

60

Do you know any Japanese businesses like this?

5

Arne: Just like Japanese businesses. We have something called *hofleveranciers*, which are companies that are at least 100 years old and service the royal family — or in the past serviced the royal family — and they have an excellent reputation, just like Japanese businesses, and I think there's actually probably a parallel to the imperial family and the services they use.

65

Male Presenter: OK. What about you, Irina?

Irina: Well, in Bulgaria we used to have lots of old-established businesses. For example, beer breweries, wineries, production of honey, rose oil. But then the political landscape shifted to communism…

70

Male Presenter: Ah, yes.

Irina: … actually, all (^{13}) businesses became state-owned. And that was actually, very sadly, the end of old-established businesses. Then, after we became democratic republic again in (^{14}), um, many people tried to revive those old businesses, in their grandparents' era, but still not so many.

75

Male Presenter: I see. That's what happened in Bulgaria.

What do you think about it?

João Orui: It also is interesting in the Japanese companies is how the owners keep
Brazil
their company alive so long, because I think, in Brazil, if the owners see
that they can…their company has the value, they will try to sell and get   80
that value for, in their pocket, so I think that it's really nice in Japanese
business that they keep continuing.

What do you think about it?

David: What's impressive, though, for me, about the long-established businesses
in Japan is they don't focus on things like infinite growth and going
global. And in the U.S., sadly, we have this focus on just getting bigger   85
and bigger and bigger, and going global and putting it (^{15}),
whereas the shops we visited, you know, they make the most beautifully-,
perfectly-crafted walking sticks and most beautiful *kimonos*. And they
really don't have any aspirations for just, you know, becoming, kimono.
com, and just going global with it.   90

6

NOTES

margin「差」 **stand out**「際立つ、目立つ」 **Harley (-Davidson)**「アメリカ合衆国の二大モーターサイクルメーカーの一つ」 **hofleverancier**「オランダ語の王室御用達」 **royal family**「王室」 **state-owned**「国有の」 **aspiration**「大志」

Useful expressions

便利な表現 ▶ **In contrast**

In contrast, in the U.S., it is large long-established businesses that stand out.
「対照的に、アメリカでは大規模な老舗が目立ちます。」（p. 4 Female Presenter）
「それにひきかえ」、「対照的に」と逆の例を挙げるときに使います。

- The book sold well last year. In contrast, the new book hasn't sold well.
  （その本は去年よく売れました。それとは対照的に、新しい本は売れていません。）
- His story was exciting. In contrast, her story was rather dull.
  （彼の話は面白かった。それにひきかえ彼女の話はかなり退屈でした。）

✳ Matching

もう一度映像を見て、以下の出演者にあう発言内容を (a)–(d) から選びましょう。

Irina　（　　）

David　（　　）

João　（　　）

Arne　（　　）

| Irina | David | João | Arne |

a. We have many long-established businesses that have been serving the royal family.

b. In my country, business owners often sell companies to get profits rather than keep them.

c. Long-established businesses in Japan attempt to meet customers' needs.

d. The products of long-established businesses in my country represent national identity.

✳ Discussion

グループまたはペアで以下のトピックについて話し合ってみましょう。

Do you think the long-established businesses in Japan will become global in the future?
Give reasons for your answer.

_____

_____

_____

7

✿ *Presenting Japan to the World*

海外の人に紹介したい日本の老舗について、以下のキーワードを参考にしながらクラス内で発表してみましょう。

English keywords	*craftmanship *historical importance *customer satisfaction *reputation	

✿ *Further Reading*

Royal Warrant of Appointment

Arne says that, in the Netherlands, there are *hofleveranciers*—companies that serve the royal family. In fact, many countries with a royal family or an imperial family, including Japan, have this kind of system. It is called a Royal Warrant of Appointment. Companies with a long history and a good reputation may receive the warrant, meaning they can  provide their goods and services to the royal family. Importantly, they can also advertise that they serve royalty, and this gives their company higher status and prestige. So, next time you buy something in the U.K., for example, look for the words "By Appointment to HM The Queen" — surely a guarantee of quality!

Write your own ideas

以下の質問に対する意見を英語で書き出してみましょう。

Besides history and reputation, what do you think is important for a company to receive a Royal Warrant of Appointment?

UNIT 2

Uniforms
制服

日本の学校やサービス産業の多くで着用されている「制服」。日本のタクシードライバーの例から、制服の着用による本人の職業意識に対する影響や外国人には制服がどう映っているのかを探ってみましょう。

PART 1 — REPORT VIEWING

日本の多くの会社や学校では制服を採用しています。Peter と Yang は、日本の制服文化を知るために街に出ます。映像を見た後に、下記の質問に答えてみましょう。

❀ Warm-up

以下の質問に対して、ペアまたはグループで話し合ってみましょう。

1. Do/Did you wear a uniform at high school? If yes, please describe it.

2. If your answer to question 1 is no, what do/did students usually wear?

❀ Vocabulary Building

(a)–(e) に対応する英訳を (1)–(5) から選びましょう。

(a) 競争する（　　）	(b) 復活させる（　　）	(c) 滑り止め素材（　　）
(d) 手荷物（　　）	(e) 素手の（　　）	

(1) luggage　　(2) revive　　(3) barehanded　　(4) compete　　(5) slip-proof material

PART 2 — STUDIO DISCUSSION VIEWING

❀ T or F Questions

映像の内容と一致する場合には T に、しない場合には F に〇をつけましょう。

1. In Algeria, there are uniforms in service industries, like in Japan.　　T　　F

2. In many countries, uniforms for taxi drivers are not common.　　T　　F

3. All of the speakers think that taxi drivers seem more reliable if they wear a uniform.　　T　　F

Uniforms

✤ *Dictation*

映像を見て、空欄を埋めましょう。

Shoji Kokami: What do you all think about uniforms in the service industry?
(Male Presenter)

> **Do you agree with Ginny?**

Ginny McKnight: I really, I really like them. And I like to be able to identify who is the
Australia worker. Because it's very crowded, especially in Tokyo, with all these
people, so you can just "Oh, it's her," or "It's him," so, yeah, in Australia
it's (^{1}) (^{2}), I think.   5

Male Presenter: In Australia, how do you identify an (^{3})?

Ginny: You have to ask
sometimes, like "Do
you work here?" or…
sometimes.   10

Male Presenter: Ah. Anis, what about
you?

Anis Boudraa: Well, the same in
Algeria Algeria. We don't have
any uniforms like these, so I'm really pleased with the service industry   15
here in Japan, with these uniforms. You can identify who is working here.
And it's also respect towards the customers because it's more professional
and more business-oriented. So I pretty like it.

Male Presenter: Do you all like them?

Nicolas Seraphin: I think, also, in my country, at least, it would tend to be, like, one size fits   20
France all. So for example you, first it's not necessarily fashionable and second, it
won't necessarily, like, fit your actual, like, body size, right. So, and, you
know, it goes along with making it fashionable, right, because if you're
gonna make it fashionable, you might as well also make it, like, nice and
fit to what, how you…so you are actually happy to wear it.   25

11

Male Presenter: OK.

Ginny: Well, even some (⁴   ) fast food chains have variations between the uniforms. So, in Japan, they're a lot more fashionable. Like, actually, um, I went to, like, a burger chain here, and I thought they were just genuinely (⁵   ). You could even wear them, like… 30

Male Presenter: The uniforms aren't the same?

Ginny: No, no, no.

Male Presenter: How are they different?

What do you think about it?

12

Ginny: In Australia it's just an unattractive T-shirt with your own pants and some kind of shoes. But here it was like, almost like a beret with a scarf, like 35 completely different, even though it's the same company.

Male Presenter: Even though it's the same chain?

Ginny: Yes.

Eddie Barth: Japanese one is really a
UK
thought-out, designed
uniform.

Male Presenter: They're obvious? With just one look? 40

Eddie: Exactly, yeah.

Male Presenter: I see. I understand that taxi drivers in uniforms are (⁶   ). Who 45 has uniformed taxi drivers? Oh, Australia?

Ginny: Just the shirts, I think.

Male Presenter: Shirts? In the U.K., you have those elegant black cabs, but no uniforms?

Eddie: I mean, maybe, I think they're so famous, those black taxis, that that in itself is almost the uniform. But the driver, it's … usually very friendly, a 50 little bit rough, and really enjoys talking to you when you get in the taxi, so what they're wearing doesn't really ([7]   ). It's about their individuality. And ([8]   ) ([9]   ) you always have to give them a big tip at the end, you know, because…

Male Presenter: I see. Then, do you think taxi drivers in uniforms are cool, or do you not 55 really care whether they wear them or not? Which?

Ginny: Definitely cool.

Male Presenter: Oh yeah?

13

What's your opinion?

Ginny: Because, they're taking your life in their hands —it makes them look more respectable. If they're just dressed in shabby clothes, do you want 60 that person driving you? Scary.

Male Presenter: Ahhhh.

Peter Macy: I think it's really
U.S.   nice when you meet
            a well-dressed taxi
            driver. In my country,
            I don't trust anybody
            in these taxicabs.
            They look, they look
            ([10]   ).

Anis: Well, I think the uniforms are cool if you consider the fact that it's more respectful towards the customers, but I doubt that if they have a uniform, they will be a better driver, or it will be safer.

Male Presenter: I see. You all seem to be saying that taxi drivers in uniforms are better. Then, why don't you have them? 75

Nour Tawk:
Lebanon
Also in Lebanon people who are taxi drivers are not really high-income people, so where you're considered it's kind of a poor class, so they don't really have the financial mean, and they don't belong to a union, so it's not like there's a, you know, a union that provides uniforms, or it's not like they can really afford to wear a nice uniform. 80

Male Presenter: I see. Anyone else?

Ji Yang:
China
In Japan, people also care about how they look. How they give the impression in front of people. But in China, just people don't care about that.

Male Presenter: That's a good point. 85

What do you think?

Eddie: Also, you need to realize that, you know, the taxi drivers' job is quite, probably quite dangerous in New York and London. And a taxi driver has a lot of responsibility for, especially late at night, you know, drunk people and violent people and stuff like that, so I think the last thing on their mind is 90 95

14

"(^{11}) (^{12}) (^{13}) (^{14})?", 'cos
you know they're gonna be wearing the white vest with the hair coming
out and big muscles, you know, it's like "You may be drunk but look at
me," you know, "You're in my cab." So I think, in Japan, of course they   100
have, you know, drunk people, but there's really not so much violence
here.

Male Presenter: OK. I see.

Eddie: I think the taxi driver is more concerned about his safety, you know, than
what he looks like.   105

Male Presenter: OK. We also heard people saying that, even if they don't meet customers,
wearing a uniform changes their mindset. Can you relate to that?

Yang: I can totally understand it. When you change the uniform, your mood,
when, change to working mood. And also you see your co-workers
working, change the same uniform as you, and also it increase teamwork.   110

15

Male Presenter: That's a point. Anyone else?

Do you agree with Anis's
opinion?

Anis: Working in an office where they never meet customers, I kind of dislike
it, because they kill all differences, individualities with other people, like
you have to look the same like all other people. It's kind of a small army,
and you just have to do your work and nothing else.   115

Male Presenter: I see.

Anis: **I kind of dislike it.** I wouldn't wear a uniform I think I…

Male Presenter: Nour, you're agreeing with that?

Nour: I would, I would be upset if I had to wear a uniform every day.
(^{15}), I would be quite upset. I like, I mean, I think many girls   120
like shopping. I like choosing my own clothes and I think that clothes
are an expression of who you are, so I don't really agree that wearing a
uniform puts you in work mode. I think for me, having a coffee puts me
in work mode, so… So, I don't think it's necessary.

Male Presenter: All right. OK.   125

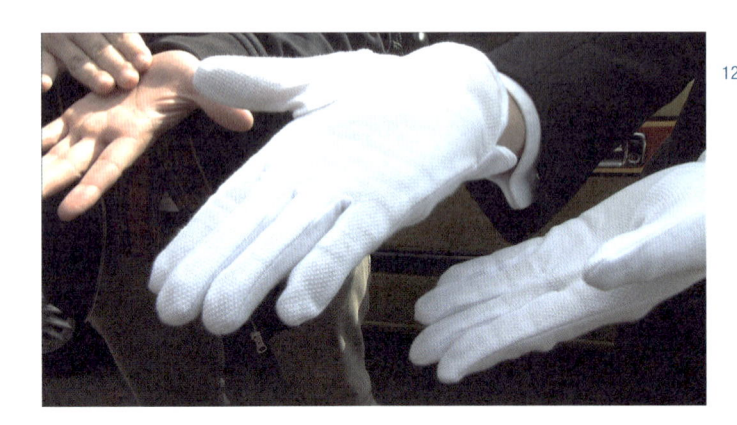

16

NOTES

business-oriented「ビジネス志向の」 beret「ベレー帽」 thought-out「考え抜かれた」
shabby「みすぼらしい、ぼろぼろの」 mindset「考え方」

❀ Matching

もう一度映像を見て、以下の出演者にあう発言内容を (a)–(d) から選びましょう。

Yang　（　　）
Nour　（　　）
Ginny　（　　）
Eddie　（　　）

| Yang | Nour | Ginny | Eddie |

a. Uniforms in service industries are good because we can identify the workers easily.

b. Wearing the same uniform as your co-workers increases teamwork.

c. What we wear is an expression of who we are.

d. In places where the crime rate is high, taxi drivers do not care about their appearance.

❀ Discussion

グループまたはペアで以下のトピックについて話し合ってみましょう。

What do you think are the advantages and disadvantages of wearing a uniform?

	advantages	disadvantages
at school		
at work		

17

 ## Presenting Japan to the World

日本人の制服に関する考え方を、以下のキーワードを参考にしながらクラス内で発表してみましょう。

 ## Further Reading

Exam Uniform at Oxford University

Oxford University has many traditions, but did you know that all students have to wear a special uniform for formal university ceremonies such as graduation, and also for sitting exams? The uniform is called "sub fusc." This comes from the Latin for "dark brown." Men must wear a dark suit and a white bow tie while women wear a skirt and a black ribbon, although there are some variations. Students also have to wear a gown and an academic cap,  sometimes known as a "mortar board." In 2015, more than 75 percent of Oxford students voted to keep sub fusc for all university occasions, including taking exams. If you visit Oxford, look out for happy students wearing sub fusc and a red flower — it means they've just taken their last exam!

Write your own ideas

以下の質問に対する意見を英語で書き出してみましょう。

Why do you think some Oxford students voted to abolish *sub fusc*?

_____

_____

_____

Volunteer Work

ボランティア

cool japan

シニアボランティアや大学のボランティアサークルなど、ボランティア活動は日本でも身近になってきました。海外諸国とはひと味違う、日本のボランティア活動の特徴について考えてみましょう。

Nathalie は静岡県三島市に行き、シニアボランティアに会い、海外でボランティア活動をする日本人の活躍について話を聞いています。映像を見た後に、下記の質問に答えてみましょう。

Warm-up

以下の質問に対して、ペアまたはグループで話し合ってみましょう。

1. Have you ever done any volunteering? If so, please describe it.

2. If your answer to question 1 is no, what do you usually do when you have free time?

Vocabulary Building

(a)–(e) に対応する英訳を (1)–(5) から選びましょう。

(a) 生産力 （　　）	(b) 派遣する （　　）	(c) 規律 （　　）
(d) 織物 （　　）	(e) 価値のある （　　）	

(1) textile　　(2) productivity　　(3) worthwhile　　(4) dispatch　　(5) discipline

T or F Questions

映像の内容と一致する場合には T に、しない場合には F に○をつけましょう。

1. In China, it is uncommon for students to volunteer.　　　　T　　F

2. It is more common for Japanese seniors to volunteer than Swiss seniors.　　T　　F

3. Korean seniors prefer to volunteer at home rather than overseas.　　T　　F

20

 *Dictation*

映像を見て、空欄を埋めましょう。

Shoji Kokami:
(Male Presenter)
I guess those activities are uniquely Japanese.

Risa Stegmayer:
(Female Presenter)
Right.

Male Presenter: Do the universities in your countries have volunteer clubs? Oh, they do! But not in France, Switzerland, or Brazil. Not in those three?

Nicolas Seraphin:
France
No, not…at least nowhere near as developed as in Japan. It would be, maybe, as Heather said, mostly for cleaning purposes, and, you know, it wouldn't be so frequent, so I would say rather no.

5

10

21

Male Presenter: They do in China? 15

Heng Xin:
China
It's usually about helping the elderly people and taking care of the young children, and also sometimes there are clubs for people to go to the agricultural, rural areas to help the farmers.

Male Presenter: I see. In Lebanon, too?

Nour Tawk:
Lebanon
Yeah, we have in my university there were lots of clubs. We had also the Red Cross, so, um… 20

Male Presenter: Ah, I see.

Nour: Yeah, for also, like, tutoring for children or, people who needed, you know, education. Many, many other clubs.

Male Presenter: There are (^{1}　　　) (^{2}　　　) (^{3}　　　)! Are they different from the university club that we just saw? 25

Heather Mcleish: Ours too, in the U.S.,
U.S.
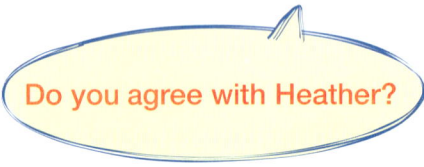
seem to be a little bit
more event-driven.
Like, every time
there's hurricanes or
big storms that come
through, then there's
a lot of organizations
where people will

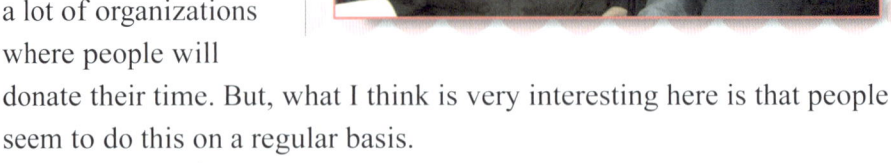

30

35

donate their time. But, what I think is very interesting here is that people
seem to do this on a regular basis.

Do you agree with Heather?

Male Presenter: All right.

22

Female Presenter: Next, Nathalie. What did you think was cool?

Nathalie Lobue: Senior citizens doing volunteering oversea work. That was really great. 40
Switzerland
Mr. Nakada-san shared his skills, very precious skills, and also work
experience to other countries, which can be like also rival countries, so I
wish Switzerland could do that as well.

Male Presenter: I see. The Swiss don't do that? Do your countries have such programs
for (^{4}　　　　) (^{5}　　　　) to share their (^{6}　　　　) in other 45
countries?

Heather: Well, we do have some, but you have more old people than we have. So…

Male Presenter: More old people?

Heather: You've a lot of old people here.

Nour: It's an aging society. 50

Heather: It's an aging society. But (^{7}　　　　) (^{8}　　　　) (^{9}　　　　) in
the U.S. is when people get to that age, they (^{10}　　　) and they go
on cruises, or they visit their grandkids…

June Sung: It's quite similar in
South Korea
Korea, too. So, after
their retirement,
they want to, like,
contribute in some
way to society. So,
usually in Korea
they do volunteer
work, like in public

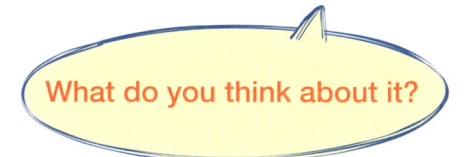

5. Modification of the meaning of 5S   55

	Ordinary 5S	Practical 5S
SEIRI	Sort and <u>dispose of</u> unnecessary items.	Sort and <u>remove</u> unnecessary items and unnecessary <u>quantity</u> from the workplace.
SEITON	Arrange for easy use.	Arrange for easy use, keep in <u>good condition</u>, and keep <u>fail-safe</u>.
SEISO	<u>Clean</u> thoroughly.	<u>Clean</u> and <u>check</u> thoroughly.
SEIKETSU	<u>Maintain high standards.</u>	<u>Prevent from becoming dirty</u> and <u>maintain good hygiene</u>.
SHITSUKE	Self discipline.	-------

The parts of underlined are modified points in practical 5S.

Ⅱ.Actual execution procedure

places. For example, like, tube station. But, the difference I felt between
Korea and in Japan is that we don't send people over other countries.
Especially for senior citizens.   65

What do you think about it?

Male Presenter: I see.

23

Xin: In China, the elderly people would more tend to, like, stay at home,
and stay with their families to enjoying having their grandchildren's
accompanying and enjoying the whole company. And, maybe they're
afraid to go abroad because of the language barrier, cultural differences,   70
so they tend to, like, to stay at home.

Male Presenter: (^{11}). Nicolas, how about France?

Nicolas: Basically, once you get, once you retire, your time, you just wanna use
your time for yourself, so…so, you know, be all for your family, so as it
was said before, maybe cruises all over the world, but also, like, seeing as   75
much as possible your grandchildren, so, yeah. Sounds very selfish, but…

Male Presenter: Japanese seniors often want to go overseas voluntarily, instead of
spending the time for themselves. Why do you think they do that, rather
than go on cruises?

Marcel Ferragi: Maybe eventual see the worlds, you know. Most of these people, they   80
Brazil
work at (^{12}) (^{13}) (^{14}), and they had
such a short vacations here in Japan…

Male Presenter: **That's true.**

Heather: They're fearless. They've, they've raised their children already. They've, they've done what they were supposed to do. And they kind of wanna have a little bit of an adventure themselves. And I think a lot of, like, everybody's life is so busy now, like, they can't see their kids and their grandkids as much as they want to. And they wanna feel like they are needed by somebody else. And it uses their mind in a different way. I think it's (^{15}).   85

     90

Male Presenter: I see.

Nour: Also Japanese people have really good health. The length of their, they stay alive for a long time, and they stay really healthy and, kind of, *genki* and energetic.

Male Presenter: OK.   95

24

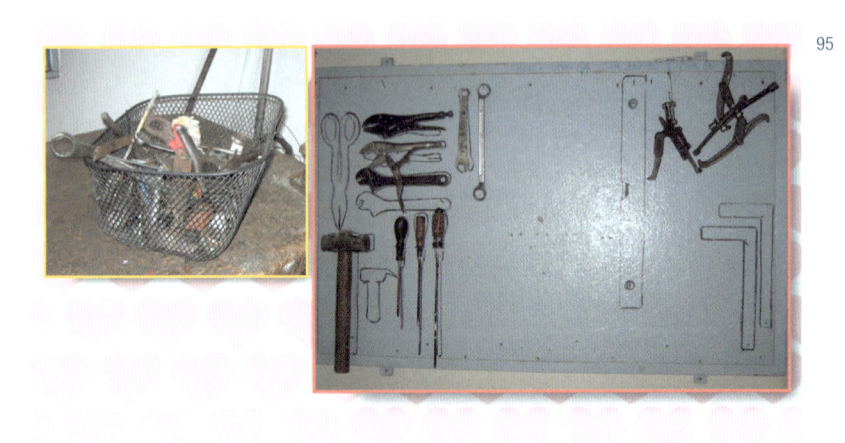

---

the **Red Cross** 「赤十字社」人道支援を目的とする国際団体　**tutoring** 「個人指導」
event-driven 「イベント駆動型の」　**tube station** 「地下鉄の駅」　**company** 「親交」

Useful expressions

便利な表現 ▶ **That's true.**

That's true. 「その通りですね。」(p. 24 Male Presenter)

「その通りですね。」と、相手に同意をするときに使う便利な表現です。

- That's true. They have such long vacations in other cultures.

  (その通りですね。彼らはほかの文化圏で長期間の休暇を過ごしています。)

- The buses are unreliable? That's true. I guess that's why you got here so late.

  (バスは当てにならないって？その通り。だから君は遅れてここに到着したのですね。)

✿ Matching

もう一度映像を見て、以下の出演者にあう発言内容を (a)–(d) から選びましょう。

Nour （　）
Heather （　）
Xin （　）
Nathalie （　）

| Nour | Heather | Xin | Nathalie |

a. Japanese senior citizens are healthy enough that they can do volunteer work.

b. I wish the people in my country would do the same things as Mr. Nakada.

c. Language barriers prevent the elderly in my country from going abroad.

d. The Japanese are too busy to see their retired parents or grandparents.

✿ Discussion

グループまたはペアで以下のトピックについて話し合ってみましょう。

What experiences do you expect from doing volunteer activities?

_____

_____

_____

✿ *Presenting Japan to the World*

外国でのボランティアを推進するにはどうしたらよいでしょうか。以下のキーワードを参考にしながらクラス内で発表してみましょう。

English keywords	*developing countries	*charity
	*natural disasters	*financial aid

✿ *Further Reading*

Helping Others

Volunteering around the world is huge. In fact, the volunteer sector is said to be a billion-dollar industry, and research shows that more than 1.5 million people volunteer overseas.

The most popular country to volunteer in is currently India. But popular volunteer destinations frequently change, and the amount of online interest in certain destinations increases greatly after natural disasters. For example, Japan was the most searched for volunteer destination right after the devastating earthquake and tsunami of 2011. The same trend was seen for the Philippines after Typhoon Haiyan struck the country in 2013.

On the other hand, there is less interest in such disaster-hit locations a few years after the disasters have occurred. People's memories fade, and the area probably appears less in the media; but often the people in the region still need help.

So, if you're interested in volunteering overseas, it's a good idea to research which regions need help most. But remember, it's not easy to fix problems immediately — volunteering is a long-term activity!

NOTES

devastating「壊滅的な」 **Typhoon Haiyan**「平成 25 年台風第 30 号」

Write your own ideas

以下の質問に対する意見を英語で書き出してみましょう。

Why do you think India is the top destination for overseas volunteering right now?

High-Tech Living (Automobiles)

ハイテク生活（自動運転）

cool japan

日本にはハイテク機器があふれていることに驚く外国人は多いようです。

現在、日本で開発中の自動車の「自動運転」を海外の人はどのように考えているのでしょうか。

Craig が「自動運転」の最先端の現場、名古屋大学からレポートします。実際に運転席に乗り、その技術の進歩に驚きを感じます。映像を見たあとに、下記の質問に答えてみましょう。

Warm-up

以下の質問に対して、ペアまたはグループで話し合ってみましょう。

1. Would you ride in a self-driving vehicle?

2. Do you think everybody can ride in a self-driving vehicle safely?

Vocabulary Building

(a)–(e) に対応する英訳を (1)–(5) から選びましょう。

(a)（周囲の）環境（　　）	(b) アクセル（　　）	(c) 半径（　　）
(d) 歩行者（　　）	(e) 障害物（　　）	

(1) pedestrian　　(2) radius　　(3) accelerator　　(4) surroundings　　(5) obstacle

T or F Questions

映像の内容と一致する場合には T に、しない場合には F に〇をつけましょう。

1. All of the speakers are in favor of auto-driving.　　　　　　　T　　F

2. The U.S. auto industry has been characterized by its safety.　　　T　　F

3. In Brazil, the death toll from car accidents is huge.　　　　　　T　　F

✳ *Dictation*

映像を見て、空欄を埋めましょう。

Shoji Kokami: Mmmm, that's great.
(Male Presenter)

Risa Stegmayer: That's what
(Female Presenter) you call high-tech.

Male Presenter: Yes, indeed.

Female Presenter: Right, so Craig, what did you think about Japanese auto-driving?

> **Are you excited?**

Craig Taylor: Absolutely (^{1}) cool. Super-cool indeed, you know. It was just,
Australia how do you say, the event in the future, of not having any crashes is just
so…something to really look forward to, as well, you know. And there 10
how do you say, like, the mapping technology, and the detail within one
centimeter, are all around you is really really amazing.

Male Presenter: That's incredible. So, what do you all think?

Nathalie Lobue: I understand the idea, really. It's all so, being like James Bond, but
Switzerland personally I don't trust machines. 15

Male Presenter: I see.

Pafan Julsaksrisakul: I wonder if this is practical. I mean, like, Japan is so systematic, and
Thailand the rules and everything is so systematic, but will this can be applied to
other places?

Jackie Mwangi: I do think first of all, for the elderly, it's really good because this is the age 20
Kenya that's really affected by immobility. So, you know, at least they have this,
and they are able to move from one place to another, that's really very
convenient. And two, in 2020, Olympics time, if they'll have launched
this, this is a plus point, because not only for, the attraction is not only for

5

29

the games as well, but for this as well. So, if you're able to be transported 25
from your hotels to the stadiums by self-driving, then that's, that's really
cool.

Peter Macy: This is great. You mentioned that you don't trust the machines. I really
U.S. don't (^{2}) other people when I'm driving. I've been hit
before, or if somebody's been drinking, you could have the mode where 30
you could just get in the car and get home safely. I think it has a lot
of uses, and I'm anxious to see where it goes. And it's (^{3})
(^{4}) in America right now, too — they're experimenting, so
this is something I'm very excited about.

Male Presenter: OK. 35

Marilia Melo: In Brazil most of the deaths are by car accidents. There is huge number,
Brazil huge number. So, I can't wait to have this one running on the streets, to
make sure it's actually become a safer environment for everybody. So, I
can't wait to have this, so you can actually read a book, you know, play
something, read your emails while you're in the car and the car is driving 40
yourself.

What do you think about it?

Jackie Mwangi: If ever they're ever in my country, I think one of the most cool thing is
you'll eventually get to enjoy a safari better.

Male Presenter: Wow! Good point.
Another thing that 45
was impressive is that
those people, midway
in their research, made
public and shared what
they had worked on for 50
three years. What do
you think about that?

Marilia: Actually very
(⁵   ). The
software world is the
same, like open source.
When you open
source, everybody
has the possibility to
give it a try, and it
actually speed up the
development, right.

Eddie Barth: I think the world is getting so small now, to do with, you know,
UK
technology that, you know, sharing any…whatever in the department
you're in, especially with (⁶   ) (⁷   ) now, you're
getting this hive mentality where you just, each human being in the world
gives one hour of their time, but you can suddenly (⁸   ) puzzles
which could never be done before.

Peter: I think that, believe it or not, I think America shares technology as well. I
think there's a lot of sharing going on with medicine and technology and
those things.

June Sung: In this world we are living in, it's really harder to keep the technology to
South Korea
yourself, to be honest.

What do you think about it?

Male Presenter: If an auto-drive vehicle became available to you, would you ride in it?

Eddie: Yeah, I would definitely, I would definitely ride in it.

Male Presenter: Of course. Well the only question is whether it actually prevents
(⁹   ).

Peter: I mean, I ride trains now, and I'm not in (¹⁰   ) of that. And I
know somebody is at the front of it, "driving" it, but it's mainly run by
machinery — the trains are. So, it's not that (¹¹   ), you know.

31

Marilia: The interesting thing about this car is that they are supposed to work in an environment that is perfect, so they have, like, lines on the floor, on the street. But in Brazil most of the streets do not even have lines, so how are they going to drive in there, right?

Craig: But in the future though, if those cars do get to Brazil, the government will upgrade everything to be compatible, so…   85

Male Presenter: And even without those lines, everything's going to be captured in the map, so it should be all right. Right? Lots of (^{12}). What are your thoughts?

Professor: The competition for developing auto-drive cars is intensifying in the U.S.,   90
Japan, and Europe, and it's supposed to (^{13}) (^{14})
very soon. The key is safety, of course. Safety is something Japan has been good at. It's what has symbolized Japan. Now the developers of auto-drive cars say they're safe because they're machines, but the riders say that because they're machines, they can't be trusted. So, the key is to   95
resolve that (^{15}). If cars made in Japan can earn the reputation of being absolutely safe, I think they can go worldwide. I want them to be available soon, but cars that are both safe and pleasurable, that you'd want to be riding in all the time, cars that typify Japan, are what I look forward to most.   100

Male Presenter: I understand.

NOTES

mapping technology「マッピング技術」 **James Bond** 英国の作家、Ian Lancaster Fleming によるスパイ小説の主人公。 **immobility**「不動性」 **hive mentality (hive mind)**「集団意識」 **compatible**「互換性のある」 **intensify**「（競争などが）激化する」 **typify**「象徴となる」

Useful expressions

便利な表現 ▶ **another thing**

Another thing that was impressive is that … 「他に印象的だったのは…」

（p. 30 Male Presenter）

一つの例のあとに、別の例を追加するときに使える表現です。

- I really like Okinawa because of its nature. Another thing I like there is the local food.

  （私は沖縄の自然がとても好きです。他に好きな点は地元の食べ物です。）

- You need a passport to go abroad. Another thing you need is a mobile phone.

  （海外へ行くにはパスポートが必要です。他に必要なものは携帯電話です。）

✿ Matching

もう一度映像を見て、以下の出演者にあう発言内容を (a)–(d) から選びましょう。

Nathalie (   )

Jackie   (   )

Marilia   (   )

Craig   (   )

| Nathalie | Jackie | Marilia | Craig |

33

a. Auto-driving will help older people who suffer from immobility.

b. The mapping technology of auto-driving amazed me.

c. Auto-driving reminds me of the exciting world of secret agents, but it does not appeal to me.

d. I don't think auto-driving can work in my country without upgrading the traffic infrastructure.

✿ Discussion

グループまたはペアで以下のトピックについて話し合ってみましょう。

If self-driving vehicles are developed, will you purchase one? Discuss the reasons for your answer.

_____

_____

_____

✾ Presenting Japan to the World

日本のハイテク製品を一つあげ、以下のキーワードを参考にしながらクラス内で発表して
みましょう。

English keywords   *cost   *technology
                        *safety   *increased convenience

✾ Further Reading

Augmented Reality

Auto-driving cars are not the only amazing thing coming to the motor industry. It won't be long before many cars on the road also have augmented reality windshields. Imagine this: as you're driving on a busy road, suddenly the car in front flashes a red color — this means you're approaching too quickly, and you need to slow down now!
Or, what if a restaurant on the side of the road turns green — maybe this means there's a special offer and you can buy your dinner half-price! You don't like the boring scenery in front of you? OK, let's turn it into a beautiful mountain landscape instead! This may sound like science fiction, but functions like these could be in your car sooner than you think.

NOTES

windshield「フロントガラス」

Write your own ideas

以下の質問に対する意見を英語で書き出してみましょう。

Besides self-driving, what factors will influence the way future drivers and passengers feel about using a car?

_____

_____

_____

Japanese Tableware

和食器

私たちがふだん家庭で使っている和食器。日本の一般家庭にある様々な形のたくさんの和食器やその使い方に外国人は驚きます。和食器にはどのような魅力があるのでしょうか。

PART 1 REPORT VIEWING

Sofia が日本の一般家庭を訪問し、家族で使っているさまざまな和食器を見せてもらいます。映像を見た後に、下記の質問に答えてみましょう。

Warm-up

以下の質問に対して、ペアまたはグループで話し合ってみましょう。

1. Did you buy your own tableware or did other family members buy it?

2. When did you last purchase tableware? Is it western style or Japanese style?

Vocabulary Building

(a)–(e) に対応する英訳を (1)–(5) から選びましょう。

(a) 箸 （　　　）	(b) 個人向けにする （　　　）	(c) 手のひら （　　　）
(d) 縁起の良い （　　　）	(e) 長寿 （　　　）	

(1) auspicious　　(2) personalize　　(3) chopsticks　　(4) longevity　　(5) palm

PART 2 STUDIO DISCUSSION VIEWING

T or F Questions

映像の内容と一致する場合には T に、しない場合には F に○をつけましょう。

1. In China, people prefer to keep tableware with the same pattern.　　　　T　　F

2. In Germany, families often have dishes that are rarely used.　　　　T　　F

3. All of the speakers think every family member should have personalized tableware.

T　　F

✳ *Dictation*

映像を見て、空欄を埋めましょう。

Shoji Kokami:
(Male Presenter)

Oh, what a great home.

Risa Stegmayer:
(Female Presenter)

Wonderful. So, Sofia, what do you have to say about your visit?

Sofia Muñoz:
Mexico

It was a wonderful experience. I learned so much. Definitely, in the future, for my own family, I would like to do that as well. Choosing dishes according to how I feel, and my mood, and everybody's mood, the season…someday.

5

10

> **What's your opinion?**

37

Male Presenter: It won't be easy. Well, what do you all think about that tableware?

Anis Boudraa:
Algeria

It's shocking. It's too much. I think in my family — it's bigger family — and we don't have that much. My family is (¹) people and we don't have that much dishes at home. So, it's shocking.

> **What do you think about it?**

Peter Macy:
U.S.

Little too much for me, right? I'm like Mexico, we put everything on one plate, and it has its own beauty, its own honest kind of (²). This looks so complicated. And to clean it all, it would be really troublesome.

15

Michael Thanner:
Germany

I…I can relate to it. In Germany, we also have dishes that we never use. They are in a beautiful cupboard, and we just have them because we like them. We never use them — maybe (³) (⁴) (⁵) (⁶) if it is a special festival. And there's a lot of that, that we are so proud of. And I think I've seen that in Japan. But I also see it in Germany. **So, I can relate to it, in a way.**

20

Male Presenter: I see. In your countries, do you have plates that are for certain kinds of foods? 25

Nathalie Lobue:
Switzerland
In Switzerland, we just have for the cheese fondue, you know, a set, that's all. But not much, not as Japan.

Male Presenter: I see.

Shi Xue:
China
As far as I know, we have oval dish for fish. So, if we cook fish, we will 30 definitely use that dish. But that's just for fish. But for other dishes, I don't think we have special dishes.

Male Presenter: OK.

Michael: In Germany, it's dependent on the sequence. You have a *hors d'oeuvre*, and then you have another dish, and then the main course, and then the 35 desserts. So, it's different dishes for each of the courses that come.

38

What's your opinion?

Male Presenter: I see. OK. Then why do you think Japanese tableware is so specifically designated according to the foods and dishes?

Nathalie: It might be, you know, the way, how in Japan, we like everything
(^{7}　　　　　) (^{8}　　　　　　), and properly, and this is for this and this 40 is for that. Might be related to that, to this little policy, Japanese kind of policy.

Male Presenter: Good point. Anyone else?

Aaron Dods:
New Zealand
I think it's also a sign of status. The more dishes you have, the more wherewithal your family has, in terms of income and social status.

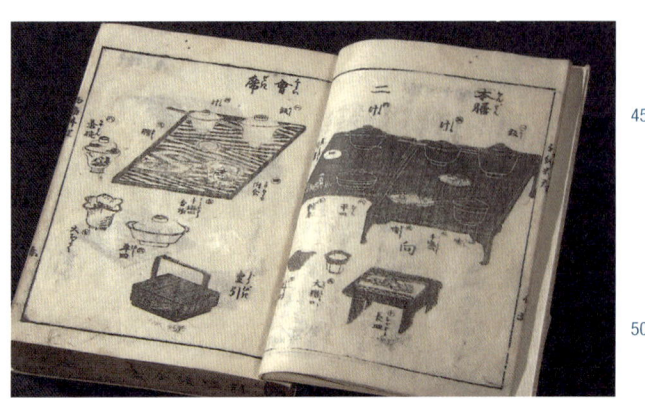

45

50

Male Presenter: OK, that might be. Anything else?

Xue: I think Japanese people see the food like a kind of presentation. So even when they…they…after they cook the food, they want to make them very beautiful in the bowl.

55

Male Presenter: In China, you have big feasts with a lot of dishes laid out. Even then, are all the plates the same?

60

Xue: I think so. We like to keep the tableware as the same pattern, especially for events or parties. That makes like, it's kind of harmony, that everything is in the same color, yeah, and shape.

Male Presenter: Oh, right. I see. We also saw how tableware was (^{9}), for the dad, the mom, and the children. Do you have that kind of custom in your countries? Who says they do? Raise your hands. Oh, you do? Uh-huh. In the U.S.?

39

65

What about your family?

Peter: Yeah. Depending on different families, of course, but dad's plate is the biggest and it holds the most, mom's plate is usually more (^{10}) and clean. And the kids' plate is, well, whatever we have left.

70

Male Presenter: Is there such a custom in Korea?

Joo Sunyi: In case of my family, my father has own chopsticks made of silver. And,
South Korea yeah, his rice bowl. Yeah. It used to be very strict, in Korea, guys…a man used some very expensive tableware…

Male Presenter: Is that still the norm in Korea?

75

Joo: Yeah, it's getting uncommon.

Male Presenter: I see. All right. In Japan, it's more than just having plates for a mom and dad. We have rice bowls, miso bowls, chopsticks, so many things.

Female Presenter: That's right.

What's your opinion?

Male Presenter: Why do the Japanese personalize all of these items? 80

Peter: (^{11}) (^{12}) (^{13}) (^{14}). But, that's the truth. That's my true feeling, because I thought about it. Japanese homes are already so small, and they use so many dishes, and I couldn't comprehend why they are doing this.

Male Presenter: Good point. 85

Peter: That's why I say I don't know.

Male Presenter: All right.

Sofia: Well, what I get is different. I get this sense of 90 appreciation and respect for each member of the family.

Male Presenter: OK.

Michael: But I think it's (^{15}). I think that there is a memory attached to each of the bowls. And you grow up, from a little kid and get older, 95 and the memory is still there. It's not about division, it's about bringing a family together and sharing a history and a memory.

Male Presenter: Oh, our theme just got larger.

40

NOTES

hors d'oeuvre「オードブル、前菜」 designate「指定する」 wherewithal「必要なお金」
rice bowls「ご飯茶碗」 miso bowls「味噌汁碗」

Useful expressions

便利な表現 ▶ **In a way**

So, I can relate to it, in a way. 「なので、ある意味ではそれを理解することができます。」
(p.37 Michael)

「ある意味では、見方によれば」と訳し、「1つの方法」という意味はありません。

- In a way, she is the most helpful in this class.
  (見方によれば、彼女はこのクラスで一番役立ってくれています。)
- I have to say that he's very clever, in a way.
  (ある意味、彼はとても賢いと言わねばなりません。)

✿ *Matching*

もう一度映像を見て、以下の出演者にあう発言内容を (a)–(d) から選びましょう。

Joo　　　(　　)
Anis　　　(　　)
Aaron　　(　　)
Michael　(　　)

| Joo | Anis | Aaron | Michael |

a. Considering the size of the family, my own family doesn't have much tableware.

b. My father has different tableware from other family members.

c. Like in Japan, we have special dishes just for particular occasions.

d. I suppose that the number of dishes a family uses might be a sign of its status.

✿ *Discussion*

グループまたはペアで以下のトピックについて話し合ってみましょう。

Which do you think is better: using separate tableware for a meal or using one big plate?

_____

_____

_____

❀ Presenting Japan to the World

和食器の良さを海外の人にアピールするつもりで、以下のキーワードを参考にしながらクラス内で発表してみましょう。

English keywords

*personalize   *designs

*stylish   *symbolize

❀ Further Reading

Silver Spoon

When you hear that someone was "born with a silver spoon in his/her mouth," you'll probably have an image of a rich, spoiled person who's never had any difficulty in life; the expression is often used in a negative way. However, choosing silver utensils as a gift for a baby has recently become more and more popular. The custom comes from the same expression above, but the meaning is to wish that the baby will be wealthy and will never go hungry. On a similar note, a wooden spoon is a sign of failure in many western countries, so even though it is popular as babies' tableware, you might want to think twice before buying it as a gift!

NOTES

spoiled「甘やかされた」　**utensil**「（台所の）器具、用具」

Write your own ideas

以下の質問に対する意見を英語で書き出してみましょう。

What are popular gifts to give newborn babies in Japan? Why are they popular?

_____

_____

_____

UNIT 6

Homemakers of Japan

主婦

育児中の日本の主婦の生活。一日体験を通じて、家庭における家事の分担を考えます。
家事や育児の分担について、海外からのスピーカーはどのように考えているのでしょうか。

PART 1 REPORT VIEWING

今回は日本の専業主婦の一日を、夫が体験してみるという実験です。どんな家事が一番大変でしょうか。映像を見た後に、下記の質問に答えてみましょう。

❀ *Warm-up*

以下の質問に対して、ペアまたはグループで話し合ってみましょう。

1. What is your favorite household chore? Rank the following 1 to 4 in order of preference.

☐ doing the dishes ☐ washing clothes ☐ buying groceries ☐ cooking

2. How many hours per day do you spend on household chores?

❀ *Vocabulary Building*

(a)–(e) に対応する英訳を (1)–(5) から選びましょう。

(a) 協力する（　　）	(b) 妊娠した（　　）	(c) 電気掃除機をかける（　　）
(d) 洗剤（　　）	(e)（用量の）1回分（　　）	

(1) dose　　(2) detergent　　(3) vacuum　　(4) cooperate　　(5) pregnant

PART 2 STUDIO DISCUSSION VIEWING

❀ *T or F Questions*

映像の内容と一致する場合には T に、しない場合には F に〇をつけましょう。

1. Some speakers believe that children should not be involved in household chores. 　　　　T　　F

2. Some speakers think it would be useful if wives complimented husbands for helping with household chores. 　　　　T　　F

3. The women speakers are all confident that their husbands can look after the housework without them. 　　　　T　　F

❋ *Dictation*

映像を見て、空欄を埋めましょう。

Shoji Kokami: I admire them for doing it so candidly for the camera.
(Male Presenter)

Risa Stegmayer: Yes. Have you ever done that?
(Female Presenter)

Male Presenter: Done what?

Female Presenter: Spend one day?

Male Presenter: Well, everyone, what did you think?

5

Sarah Tanoue: It's good for the kids to see him do it.
New Zealand

45

Collectively: Yeah.

What's your opinion?

Male Presenter: Right, it must have been a good experience for the kids. Anyone else? 10
What do you think?

Angela Schnabel: Yeah, I think it's great. I love the idea of giving a housewife or a wife in
U.S.
general a day off, especially if there's children. If there's little children involved, I think that's really great, and important.

Male Presenter: Of course. 15

Daniella Ramirez: Not only that, but for the husband to see how much the wife does in one
Chile
day, especially with two kids, and she does that every day with no help, that's…

Male Presenter: So, you heard the husband say he'll give his wife a day off every three
months. What do you think about that? 20

Sarah: It should be (^{1}) (^{2}) (^{3}).

Humzah Goolam: Yes.
Republic of South Africa

Male Presenter: Petter?

Petter Weilenmann Higashi: At least every
Sweden
month, every week. 25

Humzah: I think every weekend,
Saturdays and Sundays the wife should have a good time. She should be
off.

46

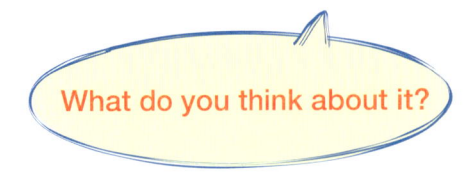

What do you think about it?

Daniella: But it's a good start. I mean, they just promise, and it's a good beginning.

Male Presenter: It's (^{4}) (^{5}) (^{6}). 30

Female Presenter: That's a good start.

Male Presenter: **If you were to leave your housework, like in that family, what would
happen?**

Haliun Hatanbaatar: I also ask my husband to cook today, and then he did, and then I had his
Mongolia
cooking, and then, like, that's very good. 35

Male Presenter: So it's natural.

Michael Thanner:
Germany

My wife sometimes travels to visit her relatives outside of Tokyo, so I take care of the household, and my daughter. I mean, I get clear instructions from my wife, which helps, you know. She explains to me how the washing machine works and… 40

Male Presenter: That's a good idea. Angela?

Angela: Yeah, so even though there is just two people in my house, if I took the day off, I think it would start to look like a single man's house. 45

There would be laundry everywhere because my husband works out during … twice a day. So, he … there is dirty stinky laundry everywhere, 50 there would be dishes in the sink, the trash would be, just, — and the cats would need fed. Like, there would be so much that need to be done, I think.

Female Presenter: In one day?

Male Presenter: Xue, what about your house? 55

Shi Xue:
China

If I go out for one day, I am just gonna be a party. So you go back home, you find toys everywhere in the living room, basically you don't, right — they don't clean the room and they go out to eat, yeah. And you're gonna find your kid didn't do any homework at all. So…

Female Presenter: So just play. 60

Xue: Yeah, it's gonna be a father-son party.

Male Presenter: I see. Daniella, how about you?

47

Daniella: He would do most of the things that he has to do, like cooking, and cleaning, and things like that, but the house maybe would not be as organized. He doesn't like drying and folding the (⁷   ) after 65 drying it, so the clothes would be washed, dried, but still in the basket, and it's like they get so much wrinkles after like…

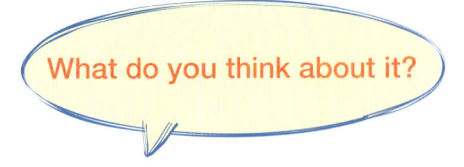

What do you think about it?

Male Narrator: Even though they said housework was shared 50/50, it seems the husbands are not all that good at it. So how do they manage?

Angela: I think part of it is also helping, like, let's do this together, code word for 70 "You did it wrong." So, let's do it together and now you know, so…

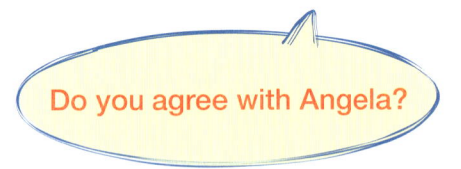

Do you agree with Angela?

48

Daniella: Yes, otherwise they get unmotivated, and they are taking the time to do it, and then you say something negative, I mean, they're not gonna ever do it again. So, you have to think about that.

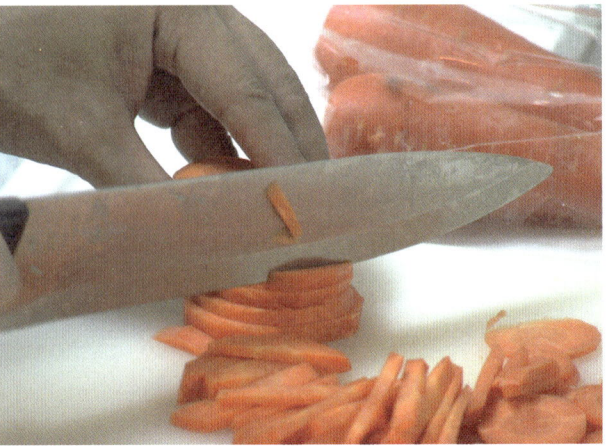

75

Angela: Together makes it better, I think.

Humzah: I just think the women should teach them.

Male Presenter: Then, Humzah, you fold your clothes (⁸   )?

80

Humzah: Yeah, I fold my clothes, like how my mom used to teach me, my grandmother used to teach me. Women should teach men how to do housework.

85

Male Presenter: Can you fold the clothes tidily?

90

Humzah: Okay, look, I mean, I wouldn't be able — because my hands are very, like, muscular, so I am not that delicate, you know. Female have an advantage. No, they have advantage and they can do it better than a man.

Angela: So, the answer is no.

49

Sarah: Well done, Humzah.

95

Daniella: You need to compliment. You need to tell them "A good job!"

Sarah: You should recognize that someone has done work for everyone, right?

Angela: You should definitely say "([9]   ) ([10]   )," and, you know, … praise…

Male Presenter: Who does that?

100

Sarah: Of course.

Male Presenter: Oh, you do?

Sarah: No, it's just common ([11]   ).

Angela: Yeah, of course, it's just like…

Sarah: He should say "Thank you," and if he does it, I say "Thank you."

Angela: Yeah, I think so. He is (^{12}) to do it. He is just (^{13})
(^{14}) good at it. That's the difference. He is (^{15})
helpful, but he just sometimes doesn't always do it correctly.

NOTES

candidly「率直に」 **a day off**「一日休暇」 **fed**「**feed**（食べ物を与える）の過去分詞形」 **wrinkle**「皺」
code word「婉曲表現」

Useful expressions

便利な表現 ▶ **If 〜 , what would happen?**

If you were to leave your housework, what would happen?「もしあなたが家事を離れたらどうなるのでしょうか？」(p. 46 Male Presenter)

起こりそうにないことや起こって欲しくないことを仮定して、「〜だったらどうなる」という問いかけができます。

- If the system were to crash, what would happen?
  （もしシステムが故障したらどうなるのでしょうか？）
- If the sun were to stop shining, what would happen?
  （もし太陽が輝かなくなったらどうなるのでしょうか？）

 **Matching**

WEB動画 DVD

もう一度映像を見て、以下の出演者にあう発言内容を (a)–(d) から選びましょう。

Humzah　(　　)
Daniella　(　　)
Xue　　(　　)
Michael　(　　)

| Humzah | Daniella | Xue | Michael |

a. We shouldn't say negative things when our partners are taking time to do household chores.

b. My partner gives me clear instructions when she is away from home.

c. Housewives should be off every weekend.

d. If I go out for one day, our rooms will be messy.

 **Discussion**

グループまたはペアで以下のトピックについて話し合ってみましょう。

When you live with someone after marriage, how would you like to divide the household chores?

_____

_____

_____

✳ *Presenting Japan to the World*

あなたの考える理想の主婦・主夫像を以下のキーワードを参考にしながら提案してみましょう。

| English keywords | *fair | *housework |
| | *babysitting | *childcare |

✳ *Further Reading*

Housewife vs. Homemaker

How do you say 警察官 in English? If you were told the answer is "policeman," you might think, "Why is it police<u>man</u>? What if it's a woman?" For this reason, it's common these days to say "police officer."

So, how do you say 主婦 in English? A lot of dictionaries still give the translation "housewife." But it doesn't have to be a woman, and you don't have to be married to do the job. So, why is it a "house<u>wife</u>"?

Actually, there is a better alternative: "homemaker." According to that term, you don't have to be married to do the job, and it is a job that either a man or a woman can do.

Changing language to show equality, to remove negative images, and to match the reality of the modern world is sometimes called using "politically correct" (PC) language.

Write your own ideas

以下の質問に対する意見を英語で書き出してみましょう。

Are there any Japanese words or phrases that you'd like to change?

_____

_____

_____

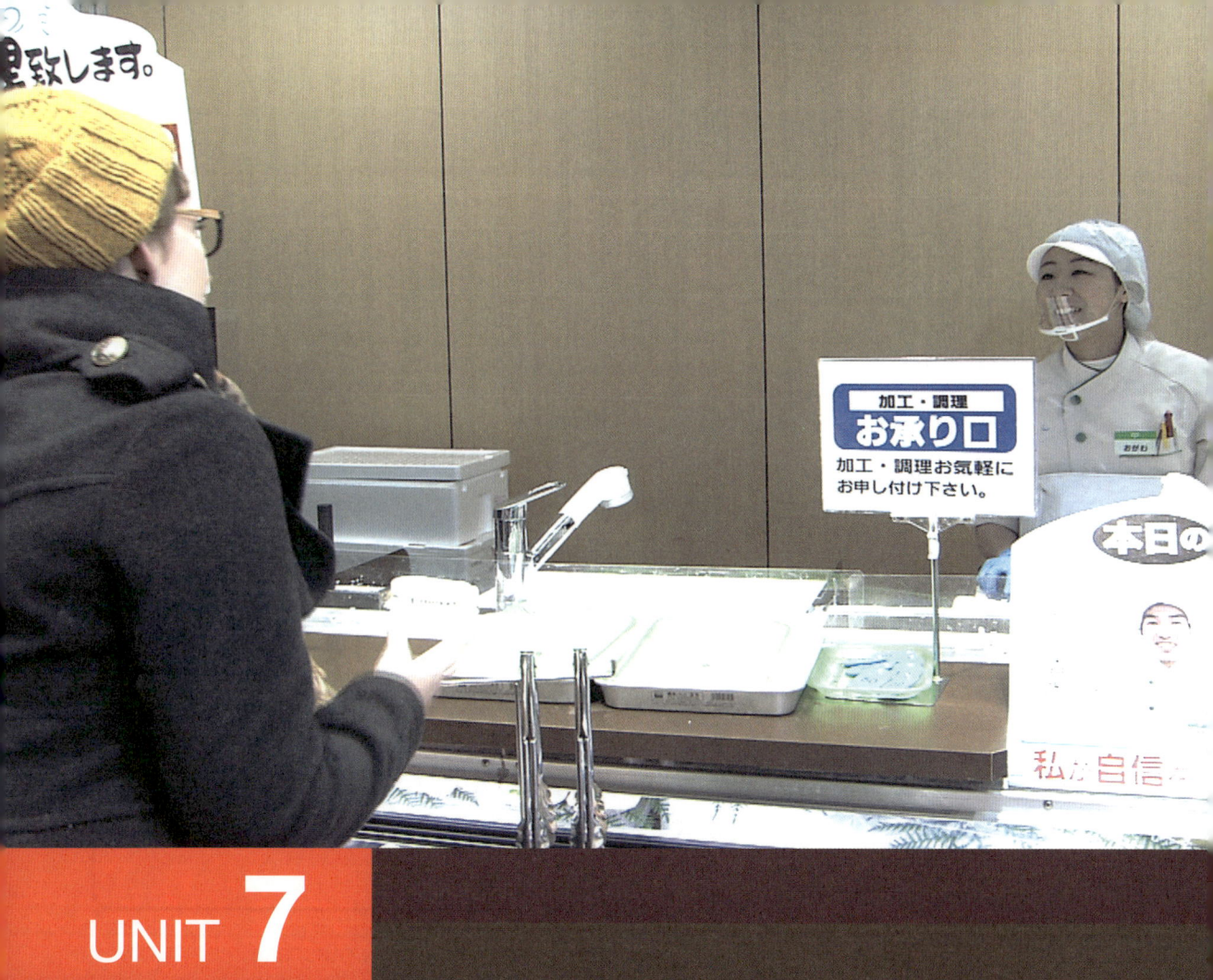

Seafood

海の幸

日本のスーパーマーケットで手に入る魚介類。切り身やかまぼこなど、使いやすく加工されている魚は外国人には人気があります。
また、魚を焼くグリルは日本特有です。外国人にとって、日本の海の幸はどう映るのでしょうか。

 **REPORT VIEWING**

Fotis と Angela が東京のスーパーマーケットに出かけ、魚売り場で売られている様々な魚に驚きます。映像を見た後に、下記の質問に答えてみましょう。

🌸 *Warm-up*

以下の質問に対して、ペアまたはグループで話し合ってみましょう。

1. Do you like seafood?

2. In English, list as much seafood as possible.

🌸 *Vocabulary Building*

(a)–(e) に対応する英訳を (1)–(5) から選びましょう。

(a) イカ （　　）	(b) 購入する （　　）	(c) サバ （　　）
(d) 手に入る （　　）	(e) 処理した （　　）	

(1) processed　　(2) mackerel　　(3) available　　(4) squid　　(5) purchase

 **STUDIO DISCUSSION VIEWING**

🌸 *T or F Questions*

映像の内容と一致する場合には T に、しない場合には F に○をつけましょう。

1. In the Philippines, fish is sliced and sold in supermarkets.　　　　T　　F

2. Norwegian-fished cod is sent to China in order to make fillets.　　　T　　F

3. In Mexico, you cannot purchase fish cut into smaller pieces.　　　T　　F

Seafood

✻ *Dictation*

映像を見て、空欄を埋めましょう。

Risa Stegmayer:
(Female Presenter)
Fotis, you went (^{1}) (^{2}) Japanese seafood. What did you find to be coolest?

5

Fotis Vlachos:
Greece
Other than the vast variety that I saw in the Japanese supermarkets, the way it's packed, presented in general, and the way they clean the fish, take the guts out, the bowels, and have it ready for instant consumption is amazing. Um, I don't think we would ever see something like this in Greece, and you know, it's just cool.

10

What do you think about it?

55

Shoji Kokami:
(Male Presenter)
Oh, thank you. You don't see that in Greece? So, all of you, what do you think about the way fish are sold in Japanese supermarkets? Is it cool, or not cool?

15

Anis Boudraa:
Algeria
Very cool.

Male Presenter: Cool? Really? Wow!

Mizhelle Agcaoili:
Philippines
Because you have it sliced already, and prepared neatly, whereas in the Philippines you have to go to markets, and sometimes the fish still jump, and I'm quite afraid of that, actually.

20

Male Presenter: Ah. But that proves that they're (^{3}).

Mizhelle: Some of them, yes. They're not cut like that.

Male Presenter: How are they sold in your countries, then? Not like this?

25

Anis: This way? No, no. You never find them…

Luz Gonzalez:
Mexico
Well in Mexico, you can buy the whole fish, or buy pieces. It depends of your taste. But here in Japan, the fact that it's already done for you, it makes easier to cook it.

Male Presenter: Hmm, I see. 30

Ginny McKnight:
Australia
Ours are (^{4}) (^{5}), I think. No bones, already (^{6}) in some kind of breadcrumbs — ready for fish and chips. And mostly white fish — no heads, no tails, no bones. Straight in the pan, so…

Female Presenter: It no longer looks like a fish? 35

Ginny: In a kind of square. So every fish, maybe it's whiting, or something like that… 40

Male Presenter: Square? Then, all you can make with it is fish and chips?

Ginny: True. We would go to like, maybe a (^{7}) to eat other fish, but to cook at home, fish and chips is, like, the (^{8}) thing.

Male Presenter: I see. Norway is a seabound country…

Cato Stromsvik:
Norway
In Norway we have, yes, it's surrounded by sea, and we have a lot of fish 45 shops and stuff like that. But I would say, maybe, (^{9}) of people they buy, like, same as in Australia: frozen fish blocks. And it's, it's really crazy, I was just reading about it actually, and they send Norwegian-fished cod to China, frozen, where they make it into fillets, and then they send it back to Europe. And this is a massive (^{10}), and it covers all of 50 Europe, basically.

Female Presenter: So it goes and comes back.

Male Presenter: Huh! Well then, in your countries, how do you cook fish? How do you eat fish?

Luz: In Mexico, you put a big frying pan, with a lot of oil and a lot of garlic. So, you put the fresh fish, it's just clean inside, and you put it whole, and you leave very very fry, both sides. And it's very tasty, because it's crunchy.

Flavio Parisi:
Italy
Usually we avoid cutting the fish before cooking it, because it's difficult. So, we just clean it up. When it's large, it's like, clean inside, and put inside maybe, like, rosemary, garlic, and olive oil, and put in the oven. It's the Sunday, like, treat.

57

Male Presenter: Huh. Then why do you think fish sold in Japan is so conveniently cut, (¹¹   ), and packaged?

Anis: The service quality, like, in Japan. It's not the only field where you find this high service quality. I mean, they make it for the customers to be easy, and also, we talked about this previously, like, for the *sashimi*, the way you cut it, it, maybe it tastes (¹²   ).

What do you think about it?

Male Presenter: Do you think all this processing is a bit too much? Flavio, you always say "Too much, too much!"

Flavio: No, no, no.

Male Presenter: **Why not?**

Anis: I wish they'd do this in my country.

55

60

65

70

75

Flavio: No. This is, this is, you know, like, perfect, like, idea of knowledge. I think 80
Japanese, you know, are alive thanks to fish ultimately, because proteins.
So I think, you know, the knowledge about, you know, these types of
animal, it gets, you know, so modernized, and it's so easy. Everybody
know about fish. And, you know, for us it's meat. You know, we have meat
treated this way. 85

Male Presenter: I see.

Flavio: We have a lot of choice. But, in Japan, not so much choice about meat.

Male Presenter: You have a point. I see.

What's your opinion?

Mizhelle: I think it's because people are very busy. And, yeah, coming from
someone who never cooked until I came to Japan, it's very convenient. 90

Male Presenter: That's a good point. You're (^{13}) (^{14}) to wait for
fish to cook (^{15}) in an oven.

Female Presenter: Or to prepare it on your own.

Male Presenter: Yes.

58

NOTES

gut「臓腑」 **bowel**「腸」 **breadcrumb**「パン粉」 **fish and chips** タラのフライに、棒状のポテトフライを添えたもの。イギリスを代表する国民的料理。 **seabound**「海に境界される」 **cod**「白身魚」 **fillet**「切り身」

Useful expressions

便利な表現 ▶　**Why not?**

Why not?「なぜ？」（p. 57 Male Presenter）
相手が否定している理由を質問するときに使う表現です。

- "I don't want to go to the party." "Why not?"
  （パーティーには行きたくないです。なぜですか？）
- "I don't feel like studying." "Why not?"
  （勉強する気分じゃありません。なぜですか？）

🌸 Matching

もう一度映像を見て、以下の出演者にあう発言内容を (a)–(d) から選びましょう。

Flavio　　（　　）

Ginny　　（　　）

Fotis　　（　　）

Mizhelle　（　　）

| Flavio | Ginny | Fotis | Mizhelle |

a. I was amazed by the Japanese supermarkets selling seafood for instant consumption.

b. In my country, fish is cut into squares to be sold.

c. Regarding how seafood is sold in Japan, it is very convenient for people who are too busy.

d. We have more choice about meat than the Japanese have.

🌸 Discussion

グループまたはペアで以下のトピックについて話し合ってみましょう。

Which would you prefer to eat: seafood cooked at home or prepared seafood at a restaurant? Why?

_____

_____

_____

59

❋ Presenting Japan to the World

外国人に勧めたい日本の魚料理や海の幸を、以下のキーワードを参考にしながら発表してみましょう。

English keywords   *fresh   *frozen
*processed   *packaged

❋ Further Reading

Superfood Seaweed

Around the world, seaweed isn't always appreciated. In the U.K., for example, it's not thought of as a food, and it's very rarely eaten.

But, seaweed has been described as a "superfood," because many types of seaweed are rich in minerals, vitamins, fiber, and protein (some types even have more protein than meat!) Also, green seaweed, such as *wakame*, is known to help prevent cancer, heart disease, and strokes.

Seaweed can be used in other ways as well. Kelp—also known as *konbu*—contains large amounts of vitamins and minerals, so it's often used as a fertilizer for crops. Carrageenan is extracted from red seaweed and is used to thicken milkshakes, cheese, and yoghurt. Agar (known as *kanten* in Japanese) is used as a kind of "glue" to make tablets. And, coralline algae (a red seaweed) is used to filter water, to make calcium supplements, and even to help with dental bone implants.

So, as you see, seaweed really is amazing. As people around the world become more familiar with Japanese cuisine, the image of seaweed will change, and the taste and the health benefits of this "superfood" will be more widely enjoyed.

NOTES

carrageenan「カラギーナン」紅藻から得られる食物繊維の一種

Write your own ideas

以下の質問に対する意見を英語で書き出してみましょう。

Why do you think many countries don't like the idea of eating seaweed?

_____

_____

_____

Voice Actors

声優

アニメ大国日本で人気のある職業の一つ、声優。日本では電化製品、カーナビなどのボイスガイダンスは機械音声ではなく声優によるものも多くなっています。日本のクールな「声優」について考えてみましょう。

PART 1 REPORT VIEWING

今回は Anis が声優の仕事場を訪問します。日本独自の声優の仕事にはどんなものがあるでしょうか。映像を見た後に、下記の質問に答えてみましょう。

 Warm-up

以下の質問に対して、ペアまたはグループで話し合ってみましょう。

1. Do you have any favorite voice actors?

2. Except for vending machines and elevators, are there any devices you would like to have voice guidance?

 Vocabulary Building

(a)–(e) に対応する英訳を (1)–(5) から選びましょう。

(a) アプリ （　　）	(b) 道順 （　　）	(c) 合流 （　　）
(d) 大人っぽい （　　）	(e) やりがいのある （　　）	

(1) merging　　(2) mature　　(3) direction　　(4) application　　(5) challenging

PART 2 STUDIO DISCUSSION VIEWING

 T or F Questions

映像の内容と一致する場合には T に、しない場合には F に〇をつけましょう。

1. No one wants to have voice guidance using the voices of famous actors.　　T　　F

2. Chinese people would like to have recorded voices for the car navigation system.　　T　　F

3. Some speakers think the ATM voice in Japan is too loud.　　T　　F

❊ *Dictation*

映像を見て、空欄を埋めましょう。

Risa Stegmayer:
(Female Presenter)

So Anis, what did you think about that (¹   ) voice acting job?

Anis Boudraa:
Algeria

So, about the voice actor, right, I thought she was very impressive and very professional. It wasn't just like giving information. She was giving information and also the purpose of the application was talking and I found it very talkative, actually. I found it cool, actually.

5

Shoji Kokami:
(Male Presenter)

Oh, what did the rest of you think?

Angela Schnabel:
U.S.

I loved it. I thought it was awesome. I'm going to (²   ) it when I get home. It was very cool.

10

João Orui:
Brazil

I'll try that too.

Angela: Yeah.

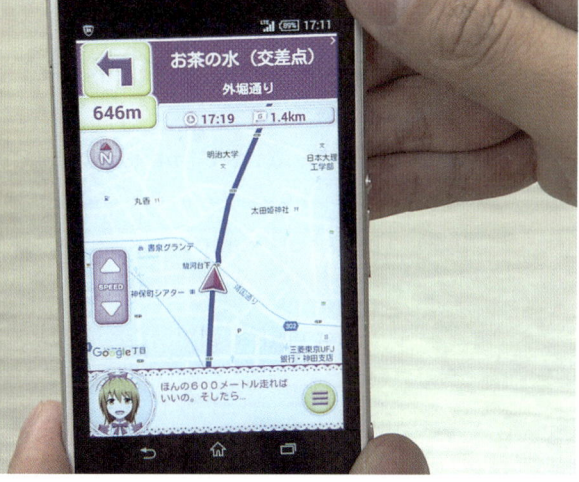

João: Is there a *samurai* mode for...

Anis: Actually, yeah, there are so many voices and that *samurai* was so cool, like "Turn left," and "Turn right," and he was giving orders, he was very cool, so.

15

Sumana Sripitak:
Thailand

That's the first time I've ever seen that kind of application. I think, like, normally, we just hear something boring like the same thing, you know, like monotone but this is really fun. I wanna try it, too.

20

Male Presenter: That's true.

63

Do you agree with Ginny?

Ginny McKnight: I think it's okay if you're walking, but driving, it's so distracting with that,
Australia like, what — like the girl's voice is so sexy, like what if you got too caught
up in (^{3}) (^{4}) her and you accidentally crashed into
something? 25

Male Presenter: That could be a problem if you get too much into the (^{5}).

Female Presenter: Yes.

Vincent Findakly: In France, too, we have that kind of thing. Like GPS with a lot of variety
France of voices, not so many that in Japan but yes, we have sexy woman voice
or we have a very famous — famous actor voice. 30

Male Presenter: So, you do have things like that?

Anis: That's very dangerous.

What's your opinion?

Male Presenter: What sort of voices were you surprised to hear in Japan?

João: I think it was for the (^{6}) (^{7}), where the bathroom
actually is. Like women's toilet to the right, men's to the left, like that. 35

Male Presenter: Okay.

Anis: I was pleasingly
surprised by the ATM
voice. So, she gives a
lot of instructions and
here in Japan, it gives
instruction and...

64

Male Presenter: In English?

Anis: Yeah, in English and in Japanese as well.

Petter Weilenmann Higashi: It's so loud though, everything is so loud.   45
Sweden

Anis: It's very loud, yes.

What do you think about it?

Petter: You don't need to know that I'm taking money out or that I am doing like — I'm checking my balance and like…   50

Anis: That's true, yeah.

Male Presenter: It's too loud. In your countries, the (^{8}) (^{9}) used for vending machines,   55
baths, shops and such, are the voices for those done by real actors?

Anis: No. Not at all, I have never seen that in Algeria.

Male Presenter: Oh, you don't have voices for those things at all? No voice announcing that the bath is ready in your countries?

Anis: No.   60

Male Presenter: No? What about ATMs? Don't they have voices?

Anis: No voices in Algeria.

Male Presenter: No voices? No voices.

Anis: Yes.

65

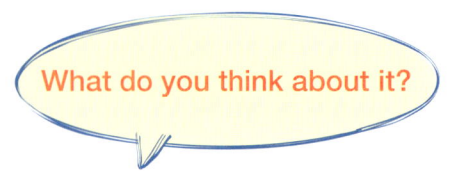
Male Presenter: Is there too much talking in Japan, do you think? Is it too much or is it considerate? 65

João: I think it talks a lot in Japan, like even the bathroom is talking to you like you...

Anis: Actually, I used to think so too, like everything is talking here. You are aggressed or assaulted all the time by voice and noises. But once I went back home, I had that reverse cultural shock, like "Why nothing is talking 70

75

here? Why there is no instruction? Why?" — so, when you get used to it, actually, it's very convenient. 80

Male Presenter: Is voice guidance in Japan cool then or (^{10}) (^{11})? Cool? Really? Really?

Angela: I like it. It's polite.

Male Presenter: What?

Angela: Yeah, it makes me feel good. It's polite. 85

Anis: It's polite, yes.

Male Presenter: Why?

Anis: Politeness is nice.

Angela: Yes, yes.

Petter: The vending machine saying "Thank you," is cool. 90

Angela: Yes.

What's your opinion?

Male Presenter: Okay. Well, as we said, these are not computer-generated voices, but real human voices. So, what do you think about most of the voice guidance in Japan using the voices of real human voice actors? How do you feel?

João: It is warm, I think. People like to hear people talking rather than robots. 95

Angela: It gives people a job, which I think is awesome.

Petter: Yeah.

Angela: Yeah.

Male Presenter: Would a car navigation system with the voices of voice actors be popular in your countries? It could become popular?

67

100

Anis: If adapted, it might. If they adapted with the language, it might work 105 because...

Male Presenter: Ginny?

Do you agree with Ginny?

Ginny: We would — if like Brad Pitt's voice or something, maybe a (¹²) actor's voice, if it was like that, we would be into it.

Male Presenter: (^{13}) (^{14}) (^{15}). 110

Ji Yang: I don't think it would be get popular in China, because we just don't care
China about the voice, what kind of voice.

Male Presenter: You don't care?

Yang: No.

Sumana: I think it would be really popular. Yeah, especially if you do like, anime's 115
voice in the navigation, like *Doraemon* or like…

Male Presenter: Oh, *Doraemon*.

Sumana: It's really big in Thailand.

Male Presenter: I might buy that, too. "Keep going, keep going. I know there's traffic, but
don't give up." 120

Anis: Because that application when you're in a traffic, she keeps talking and she
changes topic. The more you use it, the more you have more miles. And
then, she becomes friendlier,
and she changes topic.

Male Presenter: Wow, that's great. 125

Vincent: It's the thing I like about
Japan, it's just they are always
thinking about making people's
life funnier. So, yeah, I like it.

NOTES

distracting「気が散る」 **vending machine**「自動販売機」 **aggress**「攻撃を仕掛ける」
computer-generated「コンピューター生成の」

Useful expressions

便利な表現 ▶ **What did the rest of you think?**

Oh, what did the rest of you think?「なるほど、他の方たちはどう思われますか。」
(p. 63 Male Presenter)

「他の人たちはどう思いますか？」と、一人の意見を聞いた後に、他の人からも意見を求める
ときに使えます。

- I understand that Anne would like to go camping. What do the rest of you think?
  （アンがキャンプに行きたがっているのは分かります。他の人たちはどうですか？）

- We received a lot of questions from some of the audience. What do the rest of
  you think about our presentation?（私たちは何人かの聴衆からたくさんの質問をいた
  だきました。他の方たちは私たちの発表についてどのように思われますか。）

✼ Matching

もう一度映像を見て、以下の出演者にあう発言内容を (a)–(d) から選びましょう。

Vincent　（　　）
Sumana　（　　）
Ginny　（　　）
Anis　（　　）

Vincent　　　　Sumana　　　　Ginny　　　　Anis

a. After coming back to my home country, I had come to regard recorded voice
instruction as convenient.

b. For GPS, I prefer recorded voices by voice actors to monotonous voices.

c. Some kinds of recorded voices might distract drivers and cause car crashes.

d. In my country, we have GPS with many kinds of voices, including those of famous
actors.

✼ Discussion

グループまたはペアで以下のトピックについて話し合ってみましょう。

Why do you think there is a lot of voice guidance in Japan?

_____

_____

_____

✳ *Presenting Japan to the World*

日本の音声ガイダンスの良さを、以下のキーワードを参考にしながらクラス内で発表してみましょう。

| **English keywords** | *voice guidance | *computer-generated |
| | *adapt | *considerate |

✳ *Further Reading*

Voice

When you watch TV, have you ever paid attention to the gender of the voice-over actor? It seems that production companies have reasons for choosing a male or female to perform voice-over work. In advertising, female voices are often used to promote food, fashion, and medicine, whereas men are more commonly used to advertise electronic products such as smartphones, TVs, and computers. This is because these products are linked to a target consumer, frequently defined by gender.

However, recent studies show that many people feel no significant difference when they hear a male or a female voice. In one media research study, participants listened to advertisements with both male and female voice-over actors. Many participants reported male and female voices to be equally forceful, equally soothing, and equally persuasive.

Whether you believe it makes a big difference or not, the next time you see a TV advertisement, pay attention to the gender of the voice-over actors, and ask yourself, "Why was that person chosen?"

Write your own ideas

以下の質問に対する意見を英語で書き出してみましょう。

What products do you think are better for male voices to advertise and for female voices to advertise? Give reasons for your answer.

_____

_____

_____

Japanized Foreign Dishes

和製料理

日本では、インドのカレーや中国のラーメンなど、世界の料理を日本人の味覚に合わせて独自に進化させてきた「和製料理」があふれています。各国のスピーカーが、クールな和製料理について語ります。

Yang と Lingyan は、日本の中華料理店を訪れています。和製中華料理を体験し、母国の中華料理との違いに驚きます。映像を見た後に、下記の質問に答えてみましょう。

Warm-up

以下の質問に対して、ペアまたはグループで話し合ってみましょう。

1. Which do you like the best: Japanese food, Western food, or Chinese food?

2. List as many Japanized foreign dishes as possible.

Vocabulary Building

(a)–(e) に対応する英訳を (1)–(5) から選びましょう。

(a) 団子、餃子（　　）	(b) ニラ（　　）	(c) かみごたえのある（　　）
(d) 逆さまの（　　）	(e) 漬物（　　）	

(1) dumpling　　　(2) upside-down　　　(3) Chinese chive　　　(4) pickle　　　(5) chewy

T or F Questions

映像の内容と一致する場合には T に、しない場合には F に○をつけましょう。

1. In China, *gyoza* is thought of as Japanese cuisine.　　　T　　F

2. *Tenshin-don* is a local dish in Tianjin, China.　　　T　　F

3. *Ravioli* is a kind of Italian dumpling.　　　T　　F

❋| *Dictation*

映像を見て、空欄を埋めましょう。

Risa Stegmayer:
(Female Presenter)

Yes, so,

Yang, how was your outing?

5

Ji Yang:
China

Yeah, I heard some of the Japanese dumplings, fried dumplings, are very popular in China

because they are sold some of the *ramen* shop in China. So we discovered many kinds of very Japanese dumplings, like they put *mentaiko*, they put 10 *shiso*. That kind of dumplings. Yeah. They…I think they taste good. I like it. Mmm.

Shoji Kokami: So you can accept them as dumplings?
(Male Presenter)

73

Yang: Not the *gyoza* as what I think. Yeah, a kind of Japanese dish. Yeah.

Male Presenter: Do any of you have thoughts about this? 15

Yura Yefymenko: I love *gyoza*.
Russia

Pafan Julsaksrisakul: In Thailand we only eat…familiar with Japanese one. So, for me, I'm
Thailand not sure if, like, Japanese is better or not, but I like Japanese a lot.

Male Presenter: I see.

Omer Ishag: The rice was added to the meal, though. I think the *gyoza* can 20
Sudan (^{1}) (^{2}), without the rice or noodles.

Yang: The *ramen* and rice together. It's strange. Yeah.

Flavio Parisi: **Exactly.** Like you have *gyoza*. We have some kind of *gyoza*, or dumplings,
Italy in Italian food. It's called *ravioli* or *tortellini*. Basically, it's the same idea. But rice or pasta with pasta. So, you know, it's a matter of balance. 25

Male Presenter: We have a lot of opinions, but (^{3}) (^{4})
(^{5}). Oh, Omer, you have curry rice?

Omer: Yes, Japanese curry and rice is quite similar to foods in my country.

Male Presenter: Japanese curry rice is more like Sudanese (^{6}) than Indian curry
is?   30

Omer: Yes. Especially beef curry. Maybe not other curries, but beef curry is quite
similar.

> How do you like Japanese curry?

Male Presenter: How about the others? Who likes curry? Japanese curry? Oh!
(^{7}) (^{8}). Flavio, you like curry? You like it?

Flavio: Yeah. That is a good way of the Japanized food, I think. I used to live   35
in India, also, so I love Indian food. So, you know, this is something
completely different, original, and special and…yeah, it's OK.

Male Presenter: It's the same with *Napolitan*.

Female Presenter: Right, right.

Male Presenter: The same as *Napolitan*…   40

Flavio: I'm not buying it.

Male Presenter: Kelly has a hamburger
steak. Is that cool?
Is hamburger steak a
Japanized dish?   45

Did you know this?

Kelly Riley:
U.S.
Yeah, in America, if, you're not gonna just get a hamburger patty. If you're gonna get it…if you're gonna get it, it's gonna be a hamburger. (⁹   ) (¹⁰   ) (¹¹   ) (¹²   ) that we have to it is, like, meatloaf, but it's (¹³   ) different, though.

Male Presenter: This is a (¹⁴   ). You don't have it in the U.S.?

Kelly: No, not at all.

Male Presenter: No. In the U.S.?

Kelly: Hamburger.

Female Presenter: Steak? Not hamburger steak?

Kelly: No. Not that I'm aware of. I've never… yeah, it wasn't until I came to Japan, and I didn't really…

Male Presenter: Have you ever been surprised to find dishes in Japan that are localized (¹⁵   ) of dishes from your countries?

Yang: *Chuka-don* and *tenshin-don*, where they have the, like, Chinese name. But I never see it in China.

Male Presenter: We won't find *tenshin-don* in Tianjin?

Yang: No, no, we don't have that in Tianjin.

Male Presenter: Huh? Have you ever tried *chuka-don* or *tenshin-don*?

Yang: Yes.

Male Presenter: How were they?

Yang: I like it.

Pafan: I found this very weird, like, coriander *ramen*. You know, it is called here 70
pakuchi.

Male Presenter: Oh.

Pafan: That type of, like, vegetable that you put, like, very smelly, very pungent.
Yeah, but they make it a *ramen*, which I find very weird. We never have
that. 75

NOTES

outing「お出掛け」　**patty**「(肉料理の) パティ」　**meatloaf**「ミート・ローフ」挽肉をローフ・パンで焼いたも
の　**pungent**「(味、匂いなどが鼻や舌を) 強く刺激する」

76

Useful expressions

便利な表現 ▶ **Exactly.**

"Ramen and rice together. It's strange." "Exactly."

「ラーメンとお米を一緒に。それは変です。」 「そのとおり。」(p. 73 Flavio)

「そのとおり」と、強く同意するときに使います。

- "He is very honest." "Exactly."（彼はとても正直ですね。そのとおりです。）
- "Exactly. You are right."（そのとおり、あなたは正しいです。）

✿ *Matching*

もう一度映像を見て、以下の出演者にあう発言内容を (a)–(d) から選びましょう。

Flavio　(　　　)
Omer　(　　　)
Kelly　(　　　)
Yang　(　　　)

| Flavio | Omer | Kelly | Yang |

77

a. Japanese beef curry is similar to the cuisine of my home country.

b. In my country, we don't have hamburger steak.

c. It's strange to eat *ramen* and rice together.

d. Japanese curry is different from Indian curry.

✿ *Discussion*

グループまたはペアで以下のトピックについて話し合ってみましょう。

Which do you like better: authentic cuisine or localized cuisine? Give reasons for your answer.

_____

_____

_____

 *Presenting Japan to the World*

和製料理の良さを、以下のキーワードを参考にしながらクラス内で発表してみましょう。

English keywords	*local ingredients
	*Japanize
	*internationalize
	*localize

 *Further Reading*

Japanese Dishes in Foreign Countries: California Roll

Many Americans' first encounter with "Japanese" food is the California roll, a kind of westernized *sushi*. This version of the iconic Japanese food has been carefully designed to appeal to those who aren't quite ready for the idea of raw fish. It usually contains avocado, crab meat, and cucumber, and it may appear "inside-out" to people more used to traditional *sushi*, as the main ingredients are on the inside and the rice is on the outside.

Interestingly, this North America-born *sushi* roll is getting popular in Japan. Put "California" in *katakana* in a Google search, and "California roll" is one of the top autocomplete suggestions. Also, on YouTube you can find many "how to make California Roll" videos in Japanese.

So, in this case it seems that *sushi* took a trip abroad and is now coming home — only slightly changed by its experience overseas!

NOTES

ingredient「（料理の）材料」　**autocomplete**「自動補完する」

Write your own ideas

以下の質問に対する意見を英語で書き出してみましょう。

Do you accept that California roll is a type of *sushi*? If yes, why? If no, why not?

_____

_____

_____

Bags
かばん

cool japan

外国人は、日本の「カバン」文化に驚くことが多いそうです。特に、日本人の女性のカバンの持ち方や、男性がカバンを持って歩いている姿はユニークに映るようです。その理由は何でしょうか。

 **PART 1** **REPORT VIEWING**

Raffaele と Craig が、日本人のカバンの種類や、持ち方について、街で観察しています。映像を見た後に、下記の質問に答えてみましょう。

 *Warm-up*

以下の質問に対して、ペアまたはグループで話し合ってみましょう。

1. What kind of bags do you have with you today?

2. What's in your bag?

 *Vocabulary Building*

(a)–(e) に対応する英訳を (1)–(5) から選びましょう。

(a) 通勤・通学（　　　）	(b) 流行りの（　　　）	(c) だらしない（　　　）
(d) 中身（　　　）	(e) 物（　　　）	

(1) trendy　　(2) commute　　(3) untidy　　(4) content　　(5) stuff

 **PART 2** **STUDIO DISCUSSION VIEWING**

T or F Questions

映像の内容と一致する場合には T に、しない場合には F に〇をつけましょう。

1. In Australia, young women carry bags like their Japanese counterparts.　　T　　F

2. German men prefer to put things in their pockets rather than carry bags.　　T　　F

3. All of the speakers showed an interest in the idea of "bags in bags."　　T　　F

Bags

Bags

 *Dictation*

映像を見て、空欄を埋めましょう。

Shoji Kokami:
(Male Presenter)
Recently, tablet computers have gotten bigger — you know what I mean. What do you do with those? You can't put them in your pocket.

Craig Taylor:
Australia
Yeah but…hang on. I'd go back a question: **why do you want to carry that round with you anyway? You know, what's the point?** It's gonna stay in your bag all day, so why just not leave it (¹   ) (²   )?

5

10

What's your opinion?

81

Nicolas Seraphin:
France
I think, maybe, it comes also from the fact that, in Japan, you're always expected to have everything on you, like, to be ready to face any kind of situation. So, you have to have tissue, you have to have, you know, like, basically everything so that you can go, "OK, here you go," or "I'm ready for any kind of situation," and that makes the big difference. So even for men, that's why we have bags.

15

Male Presenter: Interesting.

20

Heike Brock:
Germany
For the German men it's more like, I think, they are just too practical. They don't want to carry anything around, they want to have the hands free, to do whatever they want, and they are like, yeah, so just put it in the pocket and leave. It's more like the practical thing.

Male Presenter: I see.

25

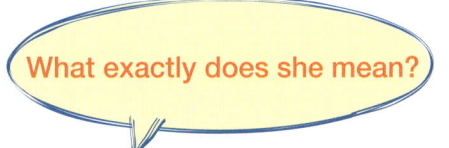 What exactly does she mean?

Raffaele Lima:
Brazil
Actually, I think it's the type of the bag. OK. If it's a … backpack, it's fine — it's very men-like. But, like, we saw in the video, like, the guy with the leather bag. That one is too fashion for a man.

Ryan Gaines:
U.S.

No, don't say…We're all human, OK? We're all human — you can have a bag if you're a man. I learned that. Really — it's OK. It's OK, really. I think all these guys here, we're (³) of having bags, because people will think we're (⁴), or something. (⁵) (⁶) (⁷) — it's a bag.

30

> **What's your opinion?**

Risa Stegmayer:
(Female Presenter)

Another question was why Japanese women carry their bags like this, on their arms. Was this question answered?

35

Raffaele: No, I couldn't. It's all beside myself. I still think this is too Japanese way of carry a bag. It's too, like…if you want to imitate a Japanese lady, I think that would be one gesture.

Male Presenter: Oh.

Heike: Actually, now I'm in Japan, I do it. I started doing it when I came here I was like "What is that?" But now I'm doing it because it's (⁸) (⁹) (¹⁰) when I want to go, for example, when I go through the (¹¹) (¹²). I have my ticket, so I can hold the bag and touch at the same time. But in Germany you don't do it.

40

Male Presenter: I see. OK. Do women carry bags like that in other countries? Oh, they do?

45

Ryan: America.

Male Presenter: America?

Ryan: American women do that.

Male Presenter: Really?

50

Ryan: This is more common, but girls do this, too.

Male Presenter: What type of woman?

Ryan: Like, the ladylike…

82

Male Presenter: The elegant ones! Elegant ladies. 55

Ryan: Like, they want to look very…

Male Presenter: They do this to look ladylike — is that what you're saying? 60

Ryan: Yes.

Male Presenter: Genteel? Ladylike?

Ryan: Yes.

Male Presenter: Oh, is that so? Same in France? 65

Nicolas: Yeah, yeah, yeah.

83

Male Presenter: I see. So, it makes them look feminine.

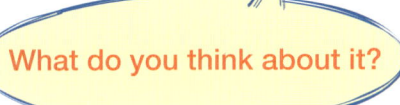

What do you think about it?

Craig: In Australia, if we do that, we are mocking an old lady. Yeah, yeah, "Yes, you know, I'm an old lady," 'cos they carry their bags like that in old…in Australia. 70

Male Presenter: I see.

Raffaele: But I have my first impression, when in Japan, it's all, like, the ladies, looks like so older when they carry a bag like that.

Male Presenter: OK.

Male Narrator: Next, let's look at "bags in bags," which are (^{13}) among 75 women these days.

Female Presenter: It has (^{14}) (^{15}) pockets, like for your seal, your pen, and your keys. If you have one of these, you don't forget things, so it's convenient.

Male Presenter: What do you think about that? 80

Raffaele: That's very cool, very cool, very convenient.

Linh Tran: Because, like, it's simple, if I have a big bag, and I put many things. So
Vietnam when I want to look for, it's like "Where is it, where is it?" something like that. So, I think this is much more convenient.

Male Presenter: You think so? How about you, Heike? 85

Heike: I think it's practical but probably I wouldn't use it myself. I always, when I go out, I always count to have everything, so I know I need to…7, 8 items that I need to have in my bag. And I always count it, and 90 then I am "OK, 7 or 8 are there," so I go out. And so I don't really need the extra bag.

84

Male Presenter: I see. Raffaele? 95

Raffaele: It's very…I really like. In a society as in Japan, like, you need things fast, like "OK, this is my card, I need to go and do the things faster," so if you have these organized, you can…it's very convenient. 100

Male Presenter: All right.

mock「ふざけて（人の）真似をする」

Useful expressions

便利な表現 ▶ **What's the point?**

Why do you want to carry that round with you anyway? What's the point?

「なぜそれをずっと持ち歩きたいのですか？何の意味があるのですか？」(p. 81 Craig)

何の意味がある？（何の意味もないだろう）と、反語的に問いただす時に使用する表現です。

- **What's the point? You pay lots of money and don't get anything in return?**
  （何の意味があるのですか？あなたは多くのお金を払って、何の見返りも受けないのですか？）

- **The invention looks nice, but I just don't get it. What does it do? What's the point?** （その発明は良さそうですが、私には理解できません。それは何をするものなのですか？何の意味があるのですか？）

✳ Matching

WEB動画

もう一度映像を見て、以下の出演者にあう発言内容を (a)–(d) から選びましょう。

Craig （　　）
Nicolas （　　）
Raffaele （　　）
Linh （　　）

Craig　　　Nicolas　　　Raffaele　　　Linh

85

a. I like having a bag inside a bag, because I can't find things easily in a big bag.

b. Some types of bag are too fashionable for men.

c. Japanese people are expected to be well-prepared for any situation.

d. I don't understand why people need to carry around too many things.

✳ Discussion

グループまたはペアで以下のトピックについて話し合ってみましょう。

What are the advantages and disadvantages of carrying a big bag?

Advantages: _____

_____

Disadvantages: _____

_____

男性がバッグを持つことが女性的と言われる国々の人々に、なぜ日本人が性別にかかわらずバッグを持ち歩くのか、以下のキーワードを参考にしながら説明してみましょう。

English keywords	*gender	*style
	*comfort	*practicality

❋ Further Reading

Bags

For you, is a bag an item of convenience or of fashion? Of course, it could be both. But, in many western societies, why is the idea of carrying around a handbag as an item of fashion somehow thought to be very feminine: for women only, not something a "real" man should do?

Maybe it's the media and entertainment industry. Grace Kelly, the beautiful actress who later became Princess Grace of Monaco, became closely associated with the Hermès bag after appearing with it in public in the 1950s. In fact, more than 60 years later the bag is still called the "Kelly Bag." And there's also Audrey Hepburn and her "Speedy 25" Louis Vuitton bag. These are iconic images that sell to the public the idea of the handbag as a fashion accessory for women. On the other hand, when was the last time you saw a famous male movie star carrying a handbag? Expensive watch and cool sunglasses — yes. Handbag? Probably not!

Things might be changing. In recent years, we've even seen a new word enter the English language: "manbag." But until we see them swinging from the arms of our male heroes, it might be a long time before they become standard men's fashion.

NOTES

Audrey Hepburn「オードリー・ヘップバーン（1929–1993）」英国人女優

Write your own ideas

以下の質問に対する意見を英語で書き出してみましょう。

What features should "manbags" have in order to reach the global market?

_____

_____

_____

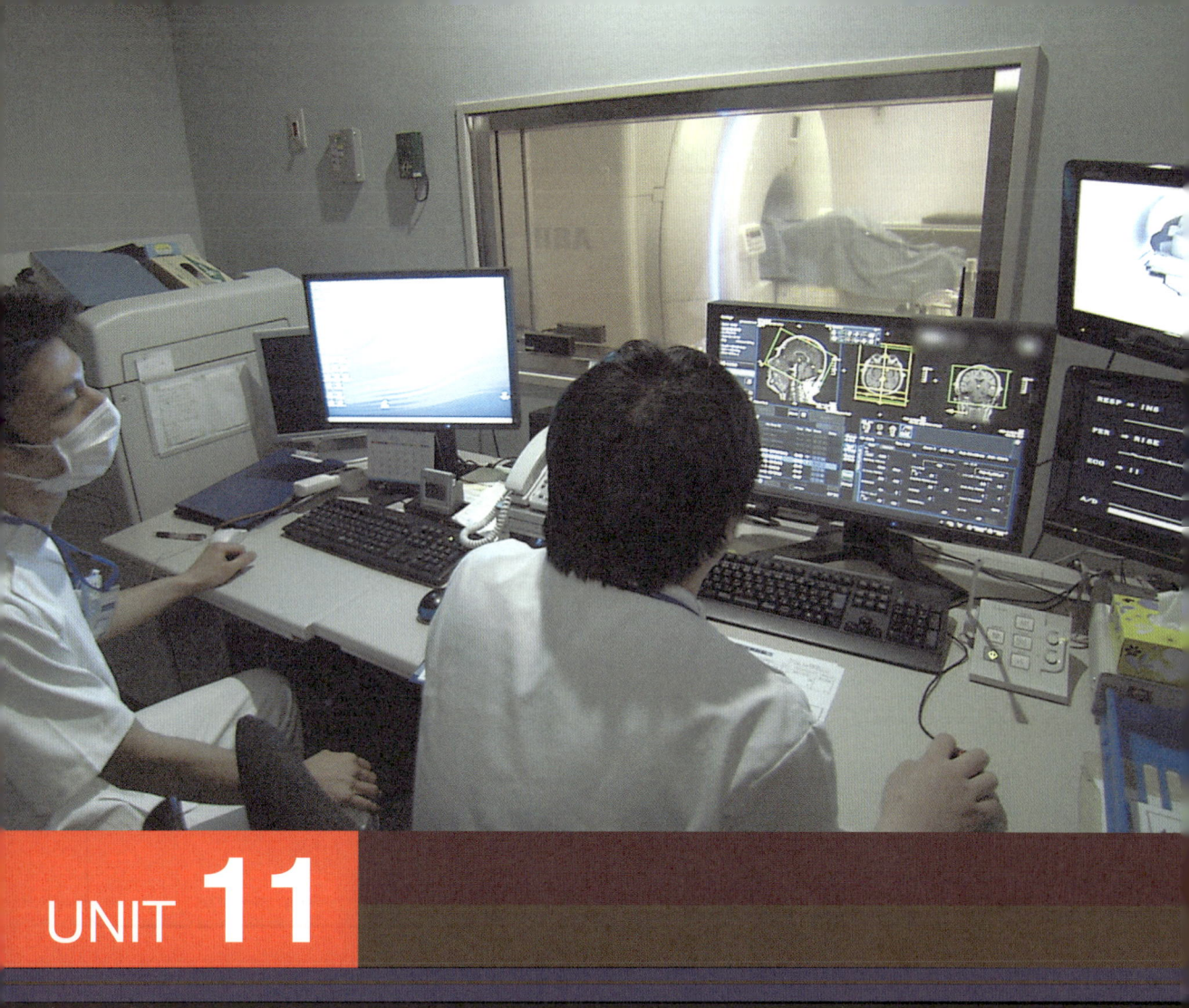

UNIT 11

Senior Citizens (Medical Checkups)

シニア

日本には、海外から人間ドックを受診しにくる高齢者が増えています。海外諸国では、日本のように人間ドックを定期的に受けることは珍しいようです。世界最長寿国、日本の健康事情を考えてみましょう。

PART 1 — REPORT VIEWING

Haliun は板橋区の病院に来ています。ここは健康診断を専門としており、多くの高齢者が訪れています が、中には中国からの受診もあるようです。映像を見た後に、下記の質問に答えてみましょう。

 Warm-up

以下の質問に対して、ペアまたはグループで話し合ってみましょう。

1. Do you have any family doctors?

2. What do you do to stay healthy?

Vocabulary Building

(a)–(e) に対応する英訳を (1)–(5) から選びましょう。

(a) 人間ドック（　　）	(b) 癌（がん）（　　）	(c) 設備（　　）
(d) 通訳（　　）	(e) 健康診断（　　）	

(1) equipment　　(2) interpreter　　(3) cancer　　(4) comprehensive health screening
(5) physical checkup

PART 2 — STUDIO DISCUSSION VIEWING

 T or F Questions

映像の内容と一致する場合には T に、しない場合には F に○をつけましょう。

1. Annual health screenings are not common for any of the speakers in
their home countries.　　　　　　　　　　　　　　　　　　　T　　F

2. All of the speakers believe that employers should arrange annual
health checkups.　　　　　　　　　　　　　　　　　　　　　T　　F

3. The Japanese have the habit of getting medical checkups from early
childhood.　　　　　　　　　　　　　　　　　　　　　　　　T　　F

✳ *Dictation*

映像を見て、空欄を埋めましょう。

Shoji Kokami:
(Male Presenter)
You know, once this show is aired overseas, a mass of people will come here.

Risa Stegmayer:
(Female Presenter)
I'm sure. So, Haliun, you made the visit. What did you think of the health screening in Japan?

> Do you agree with Haliun?

Haliun Hatanbaatar:
Mongolia
I'm pretty much surprised and with the thing that people are very, Japanese senior citizens, they are very self-conscious and self-aware, they are highly aware of their health. So, basically, it's not that really a cheap thing, but it's kind of an investment to own health. Yeah, so it's pretty good.

Male Presenter: I see. Are comprehensive health screenings like this available in your countries?

Collectively: No.

Male Presenter: No? Oh no? Really? Not even the U.S.?

Zak Elliot:
U.S.
I wouldn't say no, but it wouldn't be very common to go and get these (¹   ).

Male Presenter: Then in your countries, how do people detect diseases at the early stages?

Ginny McKnight:
Australia
She said that when you reach a certain age, you sometimes get a letter from the (²   ) or from the healthcare provider. So, they will send you, saying like "Oh you're 65, you might have, like, breast cancer or something, so please take this letter to the doctor and then you can get it (³   ) (⁴   )."

5

10 **89**

15

20

25

Male Presenter: Oh, it's free?

Ginny: But it's usually for not…unless you request it, it's not an all-over scan, it's more for just common diseases or common cancers…

Male Presenter: I see.

Ginny: It's a little different. 30

Zak: In America, maybe the feeling is more that it's not so much, like, the exact (^{5}) (^{6}) etc. that'll tell you if you're healthy or not, but you should be (^{7}) of your body and of any changes…

Male Presenter: Oh really?

Flavio Parisi:
Italy
In Italy it's the same. You always have a relationship with the family 35 doctor, so, like, usually if you have some symptoms, like, then he will prescribe you, like, a check, at the hospital. It is helped by machine eventually.

> **What do you think about it?**

90

Male Presenter: In Japan, employers arrange annual health checkups, even for young people. But how is it in your countries? Anyone have these? Oh, in the 40 Philippines. Oh. Mongolia, too? France also? Zak…no?

Zak: No, because…I felt it's strange, coming to Japan that our HR department would know what my health 45 results are. That's my personal information, right?

Female Presenter: Oh, yeah. 50

Male Presenter: I see.

Female Presenter: It's personal.

What's your opinion?

Male Presenter: **That's a good point. OK. OK, I'll change the question now.** The
number of people in Japan taking periodic health screenings has increased
by 70% in the last nine years. Why do you think that is? Why are 70%
more people taking the screenings in Japan?

55

Flavio: The more people go,
you hear "Oh, he went
there!" So, it's just, you
know, about knowing,
so it's just exponential,
I think, you know.
Like the, some people
around you went so,
"Oh, let's go."

60

65

Male Presenter: That's (^{8}) true.

Haliun: I also think that Japanese people, they don't like this kind of excuse.
Like, er, um "Oh, I feel fine." So, unless, you know, like, for example,
in my country, people will feel, like, some pain, they will go to hospital.
Even they are fine, they still go and for the checkup. So, this is very big
difference.

70

Male Presenter: Mmm. Ginny?

Ginny: I also noticed on normal Japanese television, how often they have medical
shows on (^{9}) (^{10}). So sometimes, some famous
comedians will take… "That comedian can do it, maybe I can do it too."
So…

75

Male Presenter: OK. Professor, what do you say?

91

Professor: Yes, well, as for the physical checkups and comprehensive health screenings in Japan, one factor is our governmental policy that makes us form the (^{11}) of having checkups at certain points in our (^{12}), such as 1-year-old checkups and also pre-school checkups. Another factor is that our (^{13}) organizations, from a personnel management standpoint, (^{14}) their employees to have checkups, in order to minimize sick leave and epidemics. Those factors have led to our habit, our natural inclination to take physical checkups periodically. And for early detection and early treatment of diseases, we tend to opt for the comprehensive health screening courses. By taking these courses once a year, we feel we are preventing diseases from becoming (^{15}) and making it difficult for us to continue our jobs or our social activities. I think those are the thoughts behind this trend.

80

85

90

Male Presenter: I see.

92

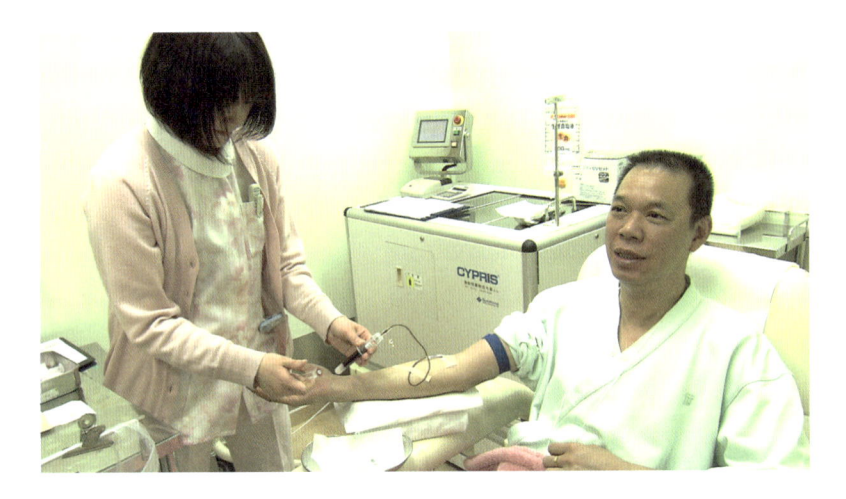

NOTES

self-conscious「自意識が強い」 **family doctor**「かかりつけの医者」 **HR department**「人事部」
exponential「（増加などが）急激な」 **prime time**「ゴールデンタイム」 **epidemic**「流行病」
inclination「傾向」

Useful expressions

便利な表現 ▶ **That's a good point.**

That's a good point. OK, I'll change the question now.

「それは良い点をついていますね。わかりました。質問を変えましょう。」(p. 91 Male Presenter)

「それは良い点をついていますね」と、良い意見を認めるときに使います。

- That's a good point. Let me rephrase that.

  （それは良い点をついていますね。言い換えてみますね。）

- I had never thought about it, but that's a good point.

  （考えたこともありませんでしたが、そのとおりですね。）

✳ *Matching*

WEB動画
DVD

もう一度映像を見て、以下の出演者にあう発言内容を (a)–(d) から選びましょう。

Flavio　（　　）

Ginny　（　　）

Zak　（　　）

Haliun　（　　）

Flavio　　　　Ginny　　　　Zak　　　　Haliun

a. The Japanese spend a lot of money on their own health.

b. Medical shows on TV in Japan are influential.

c. Employees' health results are part of their own personal information.

d. In my country, when people are sick, they usually consult their family doctor before going to a hospital.

✳ *Discussion*

グループまたはペアで以下のトピックについて話し合ってみましょう。

Do you agree that all employees should be required to have annual health checkups? Give reasons for your answer.

_____

_____

_____

日本の健康診断の良さを海外の人にアピールできるように、以下のキーワードを参考にしながらクラス内で発表してみましょう。

English keywords   *annual checkups   *health screening
                      *diagnosis   *medical technology

❊ Further Reading

Sports for Seniors

As we get older, keeping active is one of the keys to staying healthy. It's common for people over the age of 65 to spend more and more time sitting down, and less time exercising — but research shows this can have a very negative impact on health and fitness.

So, what can you do about this as you get older? Well, all you need is about 30 minutes of exercise, five times a week.

Activities such as swimming or jogging are of course great exercise for the elderly. But, engaging in social, mildly competitive sports might be better. For example, what about gateball, a sport created in Japan in 1947? There are of course the physical benefits of exercise, but there are other positive outcomes as well: social support, mental well-being, and increased self-esteem.

This kind of social sport may well be the key to staying active and healthy.

Write your own ideas

以下の質問に対する意見を英語で書き出してみましょう。

If there were a version of the Olympic Games for senior citizens, what types of events do you think would be suitable?

94

Money

お金

外国人によると日本の紙幣や硬貨は清潔、デザインが美しいそうです。クールな日本の「お金」について、海外の事情と比較してみましょう。

PART 1 REPORT VIEWING

今回は Anna が日本の造幣局に出かけ、その技術について報告します。映像を見た後に、下記の質問に答えてみましょう。

Warm-up

以下の質問に対して、ペアまたはグループで話し合ってみましょう。

1. What images are there on Japanese bills and coins?

2. What do you think are the differences between Japanese money and the foreign money in the video?

Vocabulary Building

(a)–(e) に対応する英訳を (1)–(5) から選びましょう。

(a) 造幣局 （　　）	(b) 複雑な （　　）	(c) 刻む （　　）
(d) 拡大鏡 （　　）	(e) 機密の （　　）	

(1) engrave　　(2) magnifying glass　　(3) intricate　　(4) mint　　(5) confidential

PART 2 STUDIO DISCUSSION VIEWING

T or F Questions

映像の内容と一致する場合には T に、しない場合には F に○をつけましょう。

1. People portrayed on bills are not always widely-known among people.　　T　　F

2. The U.S. coins have numbers.　　T　　F

3. All of the speakers think the design of Japanese money is beautiful.　　T　　F

Money

✳ *Dictation*

映像を見て、空欄を埋めましょう。

Risa Stegmayer:
(Female Presenter)
Right. So, Anna, what do you have to say about your visit?

Anna Schrade:
Germany
It was really impressive because I use Japanese coins every day, but I've never really had the time to look at it closely and I've never expected something like this. So, it's amazing how beautiful it is and what thought behind there is too.

5

Shoji Kokami:
(Male Presenter)
All right. What do you think about these minting technologies? What do you think, Craig? Cool?

Craig Taylor:
Australia
Yeah, same. The (¹   ), the (²   ), and how you can find that the 500 yen written — I have never seen that before.

Magnus Devold:
Norway
It was amazing, yeah. Japan is unique in making coins this advanced.

10

97

Male Presenter: Okay. Who else?

David Pavlina:
U.S.
What I like is that the anti-counterfeiting measures are also very artistic. I think other countries may not (³   ) (⁴   ) so much to the artistic value of the anti-counterfeiting measures, but I think Japan blends the two together. It's an anti-countering measure — counterfeit measure, but it's very beautiful at the same time.

15

20

> **What do you think about it?**

Male Presenter: I see. Does anyone else think Japanese money designs are beautiful? Who says yes? Oh, really? This is surprising. You are not just being nice, are you? Are you being honest?

Nicolas Seraphin:
France
As I said before, but actually our country…our currency, over the world tends to look more and more like, you know, Monopoly currency, like game kind of thing. Whereas this looks very, you know, as I would say trustworthy, very real, you know, money, ancient, that's what I like about it. 25

Marilia Melo:
Brazil
One thing I love about the coins, especially compared to the American dollars, that they have the numbers in it. Like, in the U.S. dollars, they don't have numbers. You need to read how much — which of them is worth. It is very, very hard. 30

Female Presenter: They read (^{5}) (^{6}) in letters instead of numerals.

Marilia: They don't have any numbers, so they only have letters. 35

Magnus: I think, yeah, the scenery, the nature really captured all the Japanese beauty into a small piece of paper.

98

Male Presenter: I see.

> **What do you think about Japanese money?**

Male Narrator: Do money designs reflect national characteristics? We asked the participants to show their money. 40

Jackie Mwangi:
Kenya
In my country, we use presidents. So, both the paper money and the coins, and it doesn't matter if it was a good president or bad president, he is on the money.

Male Presenter: Yeah, I see.

Jackie: But what I really think especially about the Japanese paper money is the fact that you use high — people who have achieved much. 45

50

Like, for instance, you have Hideyo Noguchi, you have Ichiyo Higuchi.

Male Presenter: Right. Okay. Who are those on your Norwegian bills? 55

Magnus: This is an opera singer, and this is a writer. I think so, yeah.

Female Presenter: They're women. 60

Male Presenter: Interesting. So that opera singers are (⁷   ) (⁸   ) figure?

Magnus: She I only heard of because of the hundreds krone bill, actually. But now they are changing the (⁹   ).

99

> Do you like the designs of Japanese money?

Male Narrator: These are the new Norwegian bills that are due for issue in (¹⁰   ). 65 The front sides have marine themes. There are patterns on the back. They are drawing high attention as being innovative.

Male Presenter: Is everyone in Norway (¹¹   ) about the designs changing from notable figures to patterns?

Magnus: I don't know. I like it to be more classic like this or even better, the yen. 70

Male Presenter: Okay, what else other than politicians?

Marilia: In Brazil, they actually have animals and nature like this.

Male Presenter: No humans?

Marilia: No. So on the other side there is a face, but this is not someone specifically, it's just a face. 75

Male Presenter: I see. All the others have politicians. The Chinese bills have politicians, Mao Zedong, and that's Lincoln.

David: Most of our currency has presidents' faces. And in fact, the U.S. is currently redesigning the bills to have more without presidents, in fact. They are looking at people like Martin Luther King Jr. and other famous (^{12}) instead of using, right. 80

Male Presenter: Professor?

Professor: Yes, Japanese money depicts nature, but it's mostly (^{13}) and that's a very interesting fact, actually. **Take the rice stalks, for example.** The 500-yen coin is similar. Perhaps it's all about the blessings of nature. 85 Rice is symbolic of Japan. There are also images of Mt. Fuji. All are beauties of nature. Our money depicts what we consider beautiful in nature. Money is something backed up by (^{14}) (^{15}), so it seems more natural to depict political figures, but this is not done in Japan, and it's quite unique. I think that the way the Japanese regard 90 money is hidden somewhere in this.

100

Male Presenter: Interesting.

| NOTES |

anti-counterfeiting「偽造防止の」 **trustworthy**「信頼できる」 **krone**「クローネ」ノルウェーの通貨単位。
Mao Zedong「毛沢東（1893–1976）」元中国共産党中央委員会主席。 **(Abraham) Lincoln**「エイブラハム・リンカーン（1809–1865）」第16代アメリカ合衆国大統領。 **Martin Luther King, Jr.**「マーティン・ルーサー・キング・ジュニア（1929–1968）」アメリカ合衆国の公民権運動の指導者

Useful expressions

便利な表現 ▶ Take ～ , for example

Take the rice stalks, for example.「稲穂を例にとってみましょう。」(p.100 Professor)
前に口述した事柄に対して、具体的例を挙げる際に使用する表現です。

- Take this book, for example.
  （この本を例にとってみましょう。）
- Take that currency, for example.
  （あの通貨を例にとってみましょう。）

✳ *Matching*

もう一度映像を見て、以下の出演者にあう発言内容を (a)–(d) から選びましょう。

Marilia　　(　　)

Jackie　　(　　)

David　　(　　)

Magnus　　(　　)

| Marilia | Jackie | David | Magnus |

a. I think Japan blends anti-counterfeiting measures and artistic values in producing money.

b. The design of our country's bills has changed and the fronts have marine themes.

c. No matter whether they were good or bad, we use presidents for money design.

d. In my country, animals and nature are shown on the money.

✳ *Discussion*

グループまたはペアで以下のトピックについて話し合ってみましょう。

What people or objects do you think countries should have on their money?

_____

_____

_____

✿ *Presenting Japan to the World*

新しく日本の一万円札をデザインすると仮定して、どんなものが良いか以下のキーワードを参考にしながらグループで発表してみましょう。

English keywords	*national icon	*nature	
	*size	*history	

✿ *Further Reading*

Money Makes the World Go Round…

We all use cash to some extent in our lives. But, how often do you really think about the money you're using? For example, can you name the Japanese author on a ¥5,000 note, or do you know what building is shown on a ¥10 coin? (the answers, by the way, are Ichiyō Higuchi and the Phoenix Hall of Byōdō-in, in Kyoto).

In fact, a closer look can reveal some very interesting features about cash around the world. It might surprise you to know that in the U.S., all six banknotes ($1, $5, $10, $20, $50, $100) are exactly the same size. In South Africa, you can see elephants, lions, and leopards on the banknotes. Even more unusually, if you rub a special $5 coin in Palau, you'll be able to smell the ocean.

So, even in these modern times when credit cards and digital money are becoming more and more common, it's still nice to appreciate the little features that make the world's coins and banknotes unique.

NOTES

banknote「紙幣」

Write your own ideas

以下の質問に対する意見を英語で書き出してみましょう。

What would be the advantages and disadvantages of a cash-free society?

Monkeys

猿

十二支の一つで、日本では「おさるさん」などと呼ばれ、動物園でも人気のある動物、猿。信仰の対象としている神社もあります。猿と日本人の関係を外国人の目から再発見します。

 **REPORT VIEWING**

Yenny と Peter が日本人の猿に対するイメージを求めて浅草、神社に出かけます。映像を見た後に、下記の質問に答えてみましょう。

 *Warm-up*

以下の質問に対して、ペアまたはグループで話し合ってみましょう。

1. List Japanese expressions and proverbs related to monkeys.

2. Divide the animals of the Chinese zodiac into those that have a positive image and those that have a negative image.

Positive image: _____

Negative image: _____

子（ね）：Rat　丑（うし）：Ox　寅（とら）：Tiger　卯（う）：Rabbit / Hare
辰（たつ）：Dragon　巳（み）：Snake　午（うま）：Horse　未（ひつじ）：Sheep
申（さる）：Monkey　酉（とり）：Rooster / Cock　戌（いぬ）：Dog　亥（い）：Pig / Boar

104

❋ *Vocabulary Building*

(a)–(e) に対応する英訳を (1)–(5) から選びましょう。

(a) 愛情のこもった（　　）　　(b) 衣服（　　）　　(c) 十二支（　　）
(d) 人気（　　）　　(e) 彫像（　　）

(1) outfit　　(2) statue　　(3) Chinese zodiac　　(4) popularity　　(5) affectionate

 **STUDIO DISCUSSION VIEWING**

 *T or F Questions*

映像の内容と一致する場合には T に、しない場合には F に○をつけましょう。

1. Some people regard monkeys as just exotic animals living in faraway countries.　　T　　F

2. Wild chimpanzees can be found in the USA.　　T　　F

3. All of the speakers have a positive image of monkeys.　　T　　F

Monkeys

🌸 *Dictation*

映像を見て、空欄を埋めましょう。

Risa Stegmayer: What did you
(Female Presenter) discover hunting for
Japanese monkeys?
Peter?

5

Peter Macy: Ah, you know, for me,
U.S. I thought, **I mean,**
this was something
really interesting,
this monkey mountain. And I learned that they call them *o-saru*, with the
"o" in front, to make it, like, polite. You know, in, in my country, kind of 10
we like bears and dogs and cats; monkeys aren't so popular. But I was
really surprised that (^{1}) (^{2}) (^{3}) kept
checking out this monkey mountain.

105

Shoji Kokami: Well, it's true. We don't say *o-zou san* when we speak of (^{4}),
(Male Presenter) or *o-kirin san* when we talk of giraffes. Japanese people probably also 15
find that interesting.

Female Presenter: A new (^{5}).

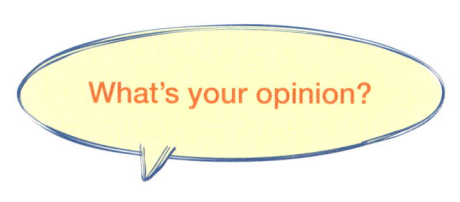

What's your opinion?

Male Presenter: In your countries, is it the same? Are monkeys popular in your countries?
And what do you think about the popularity of monkeys here?

Dimitris Kontopoulos: Well, in Greece we don't have any monkeys because the climate is 20
Greece a little bit different, so monkeys don't live in Greece. So, I guess the
Japanese, the Greek people don't like or dislike monkeys. We just

think of it as a more exotic animal. Somewhere far away, not really connected to us.

Male Presenter: I see. 25

Nicolas Seraphin: I think French people
France
wouldn't be so, like,
overjoyed by, by
seeing monkeys. So
that was really…and
the "o", as we just 30
mentioned, the "o" of *o-saru san* is actually very interesting. Yeah.

Male Presenter: Hmmm. China's different, right?

Shi Xue: Of course. Well, monkeys are popular in, in China. There are lots of
China
monkeys. And, they are one of the favorite animals. So you can always 35
find monkeys in our old stories, like, we have this famous novel…

Male Presenter: (⁶   ) to the West!

Xue: *Saiyuki*! So, we feel very close, we feel very connected…

What's your opinion?

Male Presenter: I see. When you hear the word "monkey", do you have a positive or
negative impression? What image of monkeys do you have in your 40
countries, would you say?

Nathalie Lobue: Tricky.
Switzerland

Male Presenter: Tricky?

Collectively: Yeah. Sneaky.

Yenny Sotomayor: Because they're
Peru
always, like, trying to
steal food and, yeah,
and…

45

Male Presenter: That's negative.

Yenny: Yeah, yeah, it's…

50

Did you know this?

107

Nicolas: Actually in France, we have an expression which is, which is called,
"monkey money", and monkey money means, like, fake money, basically.
So, you know, you try…

Male Presenter: Wow.

Nicolas: I think that's pretty witty…not witty, in a good way but…

55

Female Presenter: They're cunning.

Male Presenter: Hmm.

Willy Yanthy: Of course monkeys are smart, but, when someone is upset, they can say
Indonesia
"You are monkey," and it's not a good one, actually.

Male Presenter: Hmmm. Who has a positive impression? Oh, there are places with a 60
positive impression! I see.

Xue: And in China people actually choose which year they would like to have
their children. They would prefer monkey year, because that's a positive,
yes, because we have positive image for monkeys.

Female Presenter: Not the dragon? 65

Xue: Dragon, of course,
that's another very
good…

Male Presenter: OK. I (^{7})
(^{8}).

70

Xue: I think that really depends on people but really, dragon, monkeys, horses,
are bad…are very good images.

Male Presenter: Oh, amazing!

Female Presenter: In Japan, the word "monkey" generally (^{9}) (^{10})
primates, other than humans. Here we introduce some representative 75
(^{11}).

Male Narrator: Chimpanzees and gorillas live in Africa. Orangutans, gibbons, etc. are
found in Asia. There are many other kinds of monkeys. But most of their
habitats are in the tropics and subtropics, such as Africa, Asia, and South
and Central America. 80

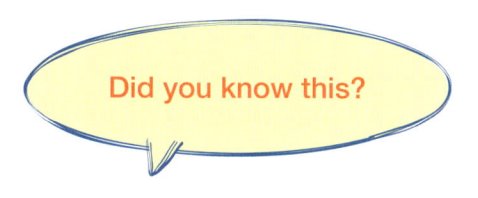

Did you know this?

Female Presenter: There are no monkeys in Europe and North America.

Male Presenter: Oh.

Female Presenter: Mmm, interesting fact.

Male Presenter: Wow, there are no monkeys in Europe and North America.

Female Presenter: Right.   85

Peter: My image of monkeys is very loud and kind of playful. All the
Japanese monkeys stand like Japanese people. They look like they're
(^{12}) (^{13}) (^{14}) (^{15}).

109

Female Presenter: Next, what aspect did you think was cool, Yenny?

Yenny: OK, so this one is when I went…when we went to the temple and we   90
found this statue. But it is important because you can see the mother with
a little baby. So, a lot of families were there to pray for fertility. Also,
they were asking for a child, for a healthy one. So, I think it's pretty cool
to have this in Japan.

Male Presenter: I see. It seems as if monkeys are pretty popular in Japan.   95

Expert: Adding an "o" appears to be used for important things inside the house, for example chopsticks — *o-hashi* and money — *o-kane*. So, we add an "o" to special things inside the house, but not to things outside the house. When you see the old picture scrolls, you can see horse stables in royal palaces, and next to them are monkeys. That means that monkeys are 100 servants of the gods that protect horses. So, you have to have monkeys next to the horse stables. This means that monkeys and horses aren't kept outdoors but are considered indoor animals. And why are monkeys with horses? Well, monkeys drive away threatening disasters and evil spirits. There's a theory that this is because the word for monkey also means 105 "to leave," so it's a play on words. The monkeys are able to prevent bad things from happening or to prevent harm from coming to the horses also.

NOTES

overjoyed「大喜びの」 **sneaky**「こそこそした」 **cunning**「ずる賢い」 **gibbon**「テナガザル」
subtropics「亜熱帯地方」 **picture scroll**「絵巻物」 **servant**「召使い、奉仕者」

Useful expressions

便利な表現 ▶ **I mean**

I mean, this was something really interesting.「つまり、これは本当に面白いものでした。」
(p. 105 Peter)

その後に、新しい情報を付け加えたり、言い直したりするために使える表現です。

- Mai is teaching English. I mean, she is a teacher.
  （マイは英語を教えています。つまり、彼女は教師です）
- I was busy today. I mean, I worked hard.
  （今日は忙しかったです。というのも、よく働きました）

❋ *Matching*

もう一度映像を見て、以下の出演者にあう発言内容を (a)–(d) から選びましょう。

Xue　　　（　　　）
Peter　　（　　　）
Nicolas　（　　　）
Dimitris　（　　　）

Xue　　　　　　Peter　　　　　Nicolas　　　　Dimitris

a. Japanese monkeys seem different from my image of monkeys.

b. In my country, we have no special attachment to monkeys.

c. We have a negative expression about monkeys, which is "monkey money."

d. In my country, people want to have a baby in the year of the monkey.

❋ *Discussion*

グループまたはペアで以下のトピックについて話し合ってみましょう。

Except for monkeys, are there any other animals that the Japanese tend to treat in a special way?

_____

_____

_____

❋ *Presenting Japan to the World*

日本人の猿に関するイメージを、以下のキーワードを参考にしながらクラス内で発表してみましょう。

English keywords	*dolls	*zodiac	
	*global popularity	*primate	

❋ *Further Reading*

Ganesh

It is not only in Japan that statues and images of animals can be found in shrines and other holy places. Ganesh (sometimes called Ganesha) is a Hindu god with the head of an elephant, and elephants are sacred in the Hindu religion. Hindus believe that Ganesh helps remove any obstacles and guides people with his wisdom. Therefore, they often pray to Ganesh at the start of a trip or new project. In Jaipur, Western India, there is even an Elephant Festival every year; elephants are dressed in colorful jewelry, cloth, and makeup, and they parade through the streets. They also take part in various games, including a tug-of-war with humans!

NOTES

sacred「神聖な」 **tug-of-war**「綱引き」

Write your own ideas

以下の質問に対する意見を英語で書き出してみましょう。

Why do you think Hindus chose an elephant to represent a wise god who can remove obstacles?

Listening (Dubbed Soundtrack)

Dictation | 吹き替え直した Listening 音声を聞いて、空欄を埋めましょう。

Unit 1 | Long-Established Businesses

Shoji Kokami (Male Presenter): Well, what do you all think about this?

Joo Sunyi (South Korea): Yeah, I think it's very nice, because there are very few long-established shops in Korea, so…

Male Presenter: OK. What do you think, Irina?

Irina Babanova (Bulgaria): It was great, actually. They adapted their product and services to the need of the customer. 5

Male Presenter: OK.

Craig Taylor (Australia): Ah, yeah, well it's one of the main ways a business can stay in business — by (^{1} _____) the customer. That's a really (^{2} _____) (^{3} _____).

Male Presenter: Yes. 10

Arne van Lamoen (Netherlands): I think this level of service is something that I miss back home. I think we used to have it, and we don't have it anymore. Japanese service is still so good that I think it surprises people.

Male Presenter: Oh, really?

Risa Stegmayer (Female Presenter): All right. Let's take a look at (^{4} _____) 15 (^{5} _____) long-established businesses Japan actually has. The board, please. Looking at the number of businesses (^{6} _____) more than 100 years, by country, this one, Japan comes first with 25,321 businesses.

Male Presenter: Wow.

Female Presenter: Yes, it is the first by a (^{7} _____) margin. (^{8} _____) 20 (^{9} _____) (^{10} _____) as many as the U.S. in second place.

Male Presenter: Amazing.

Female Presenter: Looking at the other countries, after the U.S. come many European countries. By the way, Craig's Australia is in 11th place, with 709 businesses. And Brazil, Bulgaria, and Sunyi's South Korea don't even make it into the top 20. What distinguishes long-established 25 Japanese businesses is that many are small-scale family businesses. In contrast, in the U.S., it is large long-established businesses that stand out.

Male Presenter: I see. Do you think it's cool that there are many long-established businesses, or is this not cool?

Arne: Yeah, I think it's cool. I think it's amazing. 30

Male Presenter: Really? Who thinks this is cool? Really?

Craig: Of course.

Male Presenter: It's cool? How about long-established businesses in your countries? What's different?

David Pavlina (U.S.): Well, the U.S. is a very young country, (¹¹   ) (¹²   ) 35 Japan, so our very oldest business would just be from the late 1700s. Also, the most famous are very global, international corporations. I also think that they appeal to the American sense of patriotism. I always imagine long-established businesses are things like riding a Harley, wearing blue jeans, drinking Coca-Cola, and playing a Gibson guitar or something like that.

Male Presenter: I see. Well what about the Netherlands? 40

Arne: Just like Japanese businesses. We have something called *hofleveranciers*, which are companies that are at least 100 years old and service the royal family — or in the past serviced the royal family — and they have an excellent reputation, just like Japanese businesses, and I think there's actually probably a parallel to the imperial family and the services they use.

Male Presenter: OK. What about you, Irina? 45

Irina: Well, in Bulgaria we used to have lots of old-established businesses. For example, beer breweries, wineries, production of honey, rose oil. But then the political landscape shifted to communism…

Male Presenter: Ah, yes.

Irina: All (¹³   ) businesses became state-owned. And that was actually, very sadly, 50 the end of old-established businesses. Then, after we became a democratic republic again in (¹⁴   ), many people tried to revive those old businesses, from their grandparents' era, but still not so many.

Male Presenter: I see. That's what happened in Bulgaria.

João Orui (Brazil): What is interesting in Japanese companies is how the owners keep their 55 company alive so long, because I think, in Brazil, if the owners see that their company has value, they will try to sell and get that value in their pocket, so I think the good thing about Japanese businesses is that they continue to exist.

David: What's impressive, though, for me, about the long-established businesses in Japan is they don't focus on things like infinite growth and going global. And in the U.S., sadly, we have this 60 focus on just getting bigger and bigger and bigger, and going global and putting it (¹⁵   ), whereas the shops we visited, they make the most beautifully, perfectly crafted walking sticks and the most beautiful *kimonos*. And they really don't have any aspirations for just, you know, becoming, kimono.com, and just going global with it.

Unit 2   Uniforms

Shoji Kokami (Male Presenter): What do you all think about uniforms in the service industry?

Ginny McKnight (Australia): I really like them. And I like to be able to identify who is the worker. Because it's very crowded, especially in Tokyo, with all these people, so you can just think "Oh, it's her," or "It's him," so, yeah, in Australia it's (^{1}) (^{2}), I think.

Male Presenter: In Australia, how do you identify an (^{3})?   5

Ginny: You have to ask sometimes, like "Do you work here?".

Male Presenter: Ah. Anis, what about you?

Anis Boudraa (Algeria): Well, it's the same in Algeria. We don't have any uniforms like these, so I'm really pleased with the service industry here in Japan, with these uniforms. You can identify who is working here. And it's also respect towards the customers because it's more professional   10 and more business-oriented. So I quite like it.

Male Presenter: Do you all like them?

Nicolas Seraphin (France): I think in my country, at least, it would tend to be "one size fits all," as far as uniforms are concerned. So, for example, first, they wouldn't necessarily be fashionable. And second, they wouldn't necessarily fit you well. And those two things actually go together. If   15 you're gonna make a uniform fashionable, you might as well make sure it also fits properly, so people are actually happy to wear it.

Male Presenter: OK.

Ginny: Well, even some (^{4}) fast food chains have variations between the uniforms. So, in Japan, they're a lot more fashionable. Like, actually I went to, like, a burger chain here,   20 and I thought they were just genuinely (^{5}). You could even wear them, like…

Male Presenter: The uniforms aren't the same?

Ginny: No, no, no.

Male Presenter: How are they different?

Ginny: In Australia it's just an unattractive T-shirt with your own pants and some kind of shoes.   25 But here it was like, almost like a beret with a scarf, like completely different, even though it's the same chain.

Male Presenter: Even though it's the same chain?

Ginny: Yes.

Eddie Barth (UK): The Japanese ones are really thought-out, designed uniforms.   30

Male Presenter: They're obvious? With just one look?

Eddie: Exactly.

Male Presenter: I see. I understand that taxi drivers in uniforms are (^{6}). Who has uniformed taxi drivers? Oh, Australia?

Ginny: Just the shirts, I think.   35

Male Presenter: Shirts? In the U.K., you have those elegant black cabs, but no uniforms?

Eddie: I think they're so famous, those black taxis, that in itself is a kind of uniform. But the

115

driver, he's usually very friendly, a little bit rough, and really enjoys talking to you when you get in the taxi, so what they're wearing doesn't really (^{7}). It's about their individuality. And (^{8}) (^{9}) you always have to give them a big tip at the end.   40

Male Presenter: I see. Then, do you think taxi drivers in uniforms are cool, or do you not really care whether they wear them or not? Which?

Ginny: Definitely cool.

Male Presenter: Oh yeah?

Ginny: Because, they're taking your life in their hands —it makes them look more respectable. If   45 they're just dressed in shabby clothes, do you want that person driving you? Scary.

Male Presenter: Ahhhh.

Peter Macy (U.S.): I think it's really nice when you meet a well-dressed taxi driver. In my country, I don't trust anybody in these taxicabs. They look (^{10}).

Anis: Well, I think the uniforms are cool if you consider the fact that it's more respectful towards   50 the customers, but I doubt that if they have a uniform, they will be a better driver, or it will be safer.

Male Presenter: I see. You all seem to be saying that taxi drivers in uniforms are better. Then, why don't you have them?

Nour Tawk (Lebanon): Also in Lebanon people who are taxi drivers are not really high-income   55 people, but kind of a poor class, so they don't really have the financial means, and they don't belong to a union, so it's not like there's a union that provides uniforms, or it's not like they can really afford to wear a nice uniform.

Male Presenter: I see. Anyone else?

Ji Yang (China): In Japan, people also care about how they look. How they make an impression in   60 front of people. But in China, people just don't care about that.

Male Presenter: That's a good point.

Eddie: Also, you need to realize that the taxi drivers' job is probably quite dangerous in New York and London. And a taxi driver has a lot of responsibility especially late at night, you know, drunk people and violent people and stuff like that, so I think the last thing on their mind is   65 "(^{11}) (^{12}) (^{13}) (^{14})?", 'cos they're gonna be wearing the white vest with the hair coming out and big muscles, you know, it's like "You may be drunk but look at me," you know, "You're in my cab." So, I think, in Japan, of course they have drunk people, but there's really not so much violence here.

Male Presenter: OK. I see.   70

Eddie: I think the taxi driver is more concerned about his safety.

Male Presenter: OK. We also heard people saying that, even if they don't meet customers, wearing a uniform changes their mindset. Can you relate to that?

Yang: I can totally understand it. When you change the uniform, your mood changes to a working mood. And also you see your co-workers working, wearing the same uniform as you, and also it   75 increases teamwork.

Male Presenter: That's a point. Anyone else?

Anis: Working in an office where you never meet customers, I kind of dislike it, because it kills all differences, people's individuality with other people, like you have to look the same as all other people. It's kind of a small army, and you just have to do your work and nothing else.   80

Male Presenter: I see.

Anis: I kind of dislike it. I wouldn't wear a uniform.

Male Presenter: Nour, you're agreeing with that?

Nour: I would be upset if I had to wear a uniform every day. (^{15}), I would be quite upset. I think many girls like shopping. I like choosing my own clothes and I think that clothes   85 are an expression of who you are, so I don't really agree that wearing a uniform puts you in work mode. I think for me, having a coffee puts me in work mode, So, I don't think it's necessary.

Male Presenter: All right. OK.

Shoji Kokami (Male Presenter): I guess those activities are uniquely Japanese.

Risa Stegmayer (Female Presenter): Right.

Male Presenter: Do the universities in your countries have volunteer clubs? Oh, they do! But not in France, Switzerland or Brazil. Not in those three?

Nicolas Seraphin (France): No, at least nowhere near as developed as in Japan. It would be, maybe, as Heather said, mostly for cleaning purposes, and it wouldn't be so frequent, so I would say rather no.

Male Presenter: They do in China?

Heng Xin (China): It's usually for helping elderly people and taking care of young children, and also sometimes there are clubs for people to go to the agricultural, rural areas to help the farmers.

Male Presenter: I see. In Lebanon, too?

Nour Tawk (Lebanon): Yeah, in my university there were lots of clubs. We had also the Red Cross, so, um…

Male Presenter: I see.

Nour: Yeah, for also, like, tutoring for children or, people who needed education. Many other clubs.

Male Presenter: There are (^{1}) (^{2}) (^{3})! Are they different from the university club that we just saw?

118

Heather Mcleish (U.S.): I feel in the US, things seem to be a little more event-driven. Like, every time there are hurricanes or big storms that come through, then there are a lot of organizations where people will donate their time. So, what I think is very interesting here is that people seem to do this on a regular basis.

Male Presenter: All right.

Female Presenter: Next, Nathalie. What did you think was cool?

Nathalie Lobue (Switzerland): Senior citizens doing volunteer work overseas. That was really great. Nakada-san shared his skills, very precious skills, and also work experience with other countries, which could also be rival countries, so I wish Switzerland could do that as well.

Male Presenter: I see. The Swiss don't do that? Do your countries have such programs for (^{4}) (^{5}) to share their (^{6}) in other countries?

Heather: Well, we do have some, but you have more old people than we have. So…

Male Presenter: More old people?

Heather: You have a lot of old people here.

Nour Tawk (Lebanon): It's an aging society.

Heather: It's an aging society. But (^{7}) (^{8}) (^{9}) in the U.S. is when people get to that age, they (^{10}) and they go on cruises, or they visit their grandkids…

June Sung (South Korea): It's quite similar in Korea, too. After retirement, they want to contribute in some way to society. So, usually in Korea they do volunteer work in public places. For example, like, tube stations. But, the difference I felt between Korea and Japan is that we don't send people to other countries. Especially senior citizens.

40

Male Presenter: I see.

Xin: In China, the elderly people would more tend to stay at home, and stay with their families to enjoy spending time with their grandchildren accompanied and enjoying the whole company. And, maybe they're afraid to go abroad because of the language barrier, cultural differences, so they tend to stay at home.

45

Male Presenter: (¹¹   ). Nicolas, how about France?

Nicolas: Basically, once you retire, you just wanna use your time for yourself, so…, you know, be with your family, as it was said before, maybe cruises all over the world, but also seeing your grandchildren as much as possible, so, yeah. Sounds very selfish, but…

Male Presenter: Japanese seniors often want to go overseas voluntarily, instead of spending the time for themselves. Why do you think they do that, rather than go on cruises?

50

Marcel Ferragi (Brazil): Maybe to finally see the world, you know. Most of these people, they work (¹²   ) (¹³   ) (¹⁴   ), and they had such short vacations here in Japan…

Male Presenter: That's true.

55

Heather: They're fearless. They've raised their children already. They've done what they were supposed to do. And they wanna have a little bit of an adventure themselves. And I think everybody's life is so busy now, they can't see their kids and their grandkids as much as they want to. And they wanna feel like they are needed by somebody else. And it uses their mind in a different way. I think it's (¹⁵   ).

119

60

Male Presenter: I see.

Nour: Also Japanese people have really good health. They stay alive for a long time, and they stay really healthy and *genki* and energetic.

Male Presenter: OK.

Shoji Kokami (Male Presenter): Mmmm, that's great.

Risa Stegmayer (Female Presenter): That's what you call hi-tech.

Male Presenter: Yes, indeed.

Female Presenter: Right, so Craig, what did you think about Japanese auto-driving?

Craig Taylor (Australia): Absolutely (^{1}) cool. Super-cool indeed. It was just, how can 5 you say, in the future, not having any crashes is just something to really look forward to. And the mapping technology, and the detail within one centimeter, are all around you. It's really really amazing.

Male Presenter: That's incredible. So, what do you all think?

Nathalie Lobue (Switzerland): I understand the idea, really. It's just like a James Bond movie, 10 but personally I don't trust machines.

Male Presenter: I see.

Pafan Julsaksrisakul (Thailand): I wonder if this is practical. I mean, like, Japan is so systematic, and the rules and everything are so systematic, but can this be applied to other places? 15

Jackie Mwangi (Kenya): I do think first of all, for the elderly, it's really good because this is the age group that's really affected by immobility. So, you know, at least they have this, and they are able to move from one place to another, that's really very convenient. And two, in 2020, Olympics time, if they'll have launched this, this is a plus point, because not only will the games be an attraction, but this will be as well. So, if you're able to be transported from your 20 hotel to the stadiums by self-driving, then that's really cool.

Peter Macy (U.S.): This is great. You mentioned that you don't trust machines. I really don't (^{2}) other people when I'm driving. I've been hit before, or if you've been drinking, you could have the mode where you could just get in the car and get home safely. I think it has a lot of uses, and I'm curious to see where it goes. And it's (^{3}) (^{4}) in 25 America right now, too — they're experimenting, so this is something I'm very excited about.

Male Presenter: OK.

Marilia Melo (Brazil): So, in Brazil most deaths are by car accidents. There is a huge number, huge number. So, I can't wait to have this system running on the streets, to make sure it's actually become a safer environment for everybody. So, I can't wait to have this, so you can actually read 30 a book, you know, check your emails while you're in the car and the car is driving itself.

Jackie: If they're ever in my country, I think one of the coolest things is you'll eventually get to enjoy a safari better.

Male Presenter: Wow! Good point. Another thing that was impressive is that those people, midway in their research, made public and shared what they had worked on for three years. What 35 do you think about that?

Marilia: It's actually very (^{5}). The software world is the same, like open source. When you have open source, everybody has the possibility to give it a try, and it actually speeds up the development, right.

Eddie Barth (UK): I think the world is getting so small now, with, you know, technology.   40 Whatever department you're in, especially with (^{6}) (^{7})now, you're getting this hive mentality where each human being in the world gives one hour of their time, but you can suddenly (^{8}) puzzles which could never be done before.

Peter: I think that. Believe it or not, I think America shares technology as well. I think there's a lot of sharing going on with medicine and technology and those things.   45

June Sung (South Korea): In the world we are living in, it is really harder to keep technology to yourself, to be honest.

Male Presenter: If an auto-drive vehicle became available to you, would you ride in it?

Eddie: Yeah, I would definitely, I would definitely ride in it.

Male Presenter: Of course. Well the only question is whether it actually prevents (^{9}).   50

Peter: But I mean, I ride trains now, and I'm not in (^{10}) of that. And I know somebody is at the front of it, "driving" it, but it's mainly run by machinery — the trains are. So, it's not that (^{11}), you know.

Marilia: The interesting thing about these cars is that they are supposed to work in an environment that is perfect, so they have, like, lines on the street. But in Brazil most of the streets do not even   55 have lines, so how are they going to drive there, right?

121

Craig: But in the future though, if those cars do get to Brazil, the government will upgrade everything to be compatible, so…

Male Presenter: And even without those lines, everything's going to be captured in the map, so it should be all right. Right? Lots of (^{12}). What are your thoughts?   60

Professor: The competition for developing auto-drive cars is intensifying in the U.S., Japan, and Europe, and it's supposed to (^{13}) (^{14}) very soon. The key is safety, of course. Safety is something Japan has been good at. It's what has symbolized Japan. Now the developers of auto-drive cars say they're safe because they're machines, but the riders say that because they're machines, they can't be trusted. So, the key is to resolve that (^{15}).   65 If cars made in Japan can earn the reputation of being absolutely safe, I think they can go worldwide. I want them to be available soon, but cars that are both safe and pleasurable, that you'd want to be riding in all the time, cars that typify Japan, are what I look forward to most.

Male Presenter: I understand.

Shoji Kokami (Male Presenter): Oh, what a great home.

Risa Stegmayer (Female Presenter): Wonderful. So, Sofia, what do you have to say about your visit?

Sofia Muñoz (Mexico): It was a wonderful experience. I learned so much. Definitely, in the future, for my own family, I would like to do that as well. Choosing dishes according to how I feel, and my mood, and everybody's mood, the season…someday. 5

Male Presenter: It won't be easy. Well, what do you all think about that tableware?

Anis Boudraa (Algeria): It's shocking. It's too much. I think in my family -- it's a bigger family -- and we don't have that much. My family is (^{1}) people and we don't have that many dishes at home. So, it's shocking. 10

Peter Macy (U.S.): A little too much for me, right. Like in Mexico, we put everything on one plate, and it has its own beauty, its own honest kind of (^{2}). This looks so complicated. And to clean it all, it would be really troublesome.

Michael Thanner (Germany): I can relate to it. In Germany, we also have dishes that we never use. They are in a beautiful cupboard, and we just have them because we like them. We never use 15 them - maybe (^{3}) (^{4}) (^{5}) (^{6}) if it is a special festival. And there's a lot of that, which we are so proud of. And I think I've seen that in Japan. But I also see it in Germany. So, I can relate to it, in a way.

Male Presenter: I see. In your countries, do you have plates that are for certain kinds of foods?

Nathalie Lobue (Switzerland): In Switzerland, we just have special plates for cheese fondue, you 20 know, a set, that's all. But not so many, not like Japan.

Male Presenter: I see.

Shi Xue (China): As far as I know, we have a special dish for fish. So, if we cook fish, we will definitely use that dish. But that's just for fish. But for other food, I don't think we have special dishes. 25

Male Presenter: OK.

Michael: In Germany, it's dependent on the sequence. You have an *hors d'oeuvre*, and then you have another dish, and then the main course, and then the dessert. So, it's different dishes for each of the courses that come.

Male Presenter: I see. OK. Then why do you think Japanese tableware is so specifically 30 designated according to the foods and dishes?

Nathalie: It might be because Japanese people like everything to be (^{7}) (^{8}) and proper, and this is for this and this is for that. It might be related to that, to this way of thinking, Japanese way of thinking.

Male Presenter: Good point. Anyone else? 35

Aaron Dods (New Zealand): I think it's also a sign of status. The more dishes you have, the more your family has, in terms of income and social status.

Male Presenter: OK, that might be. Anything else?

Xue: I think Japanese people see food as like a kind of presentation. So even after they cook the food, they want to make it very beautiful in the bowl. 40

Male Presenter: In China, you have big feasts with a lot of dishes laid out. Even then, are all the plates the same?

Xue: I think so. We like to keep the tableware the same pattern, especially for events or parties. That makes it kind of a harmony, that everything is the same color, and shape.

Male Presenter: Oh, right. I see. We also saw how tableware was (^{9}), for the dad, 45 the mom, and the children. Do you have that kind of custom in your countries? Who says they do? Raise your hands. Oh, you do? Uh-huh. In the U.S.?

Peter: Yeah. It depends on different families, of course, but dad's plate is the biggest and it holds the most, mom's plate is usually more (^{10}) and clean. And the kids' plate is, well, whatever we have left. 50

Male Presenter: Is there such a custom in Korea?

Joo Sunyi (South Korea): In the case of my family, my father has his own chopsticks made of silver, and his rice bowl. It used to be very strict, in Korea men used some very expensive tableware…

Male Presenter: Is that still the norm in Korea? 55

Joo: It's getting less common.

Male Presenter: I see. All right. In Japan, it's more than just having plates for mom and dad. We have rice bowls, miso bowls, chopsticks, so many things.

123

Female Presenter: That's right.

Male Presenter: Why do the Japanese personalize all of these items? 60

Peter: (^{11}) (^{12}) (^{13}) (^{14}). But, that's the truth. That's my true feeling, because I thought about it. Japanese homes are already so small, and they use so many dishes, and I couldn't comprehend why they are doing this.

Male Presenter: Good point.

Peter: So that's why I say I don't know. 65

Male Presenter: All right.

Sofia: Well, what I get is different. I get a sense of appreciation and respect for each member of the family.

Male Presenter: OK.

Michael: But I think it's (^{15}). I think there is a memory attached to each of the bowls. 70 And you grow up, from a little kid and get older, and the memory is still there. It's not about division, it's about bringing a family together and sharing a history and a memory.

Male Presenter: Oh, our theme just got larger.

Unit 6 Homemakers of Japan

Shoji Kokami (Male Presenter): I admire them for doing it so candidly for the camera.

Risa Stegmayer (Female Presenter): Yes. Have you ever done that?

Male Presenter: Done what?

Female Presenter: Spend one day?

Male Presenter: Well, everyone, what did you think? 5

Sarah Tanoue (New Zealand): It is good for the kids to see him do it.

Collectively: Yes.

Male Presenter: Right, it must have been a good experience for the kids. Anyone else? What do you think?

Angela Schnabel (U.S.): Yes, I think it is great. I love the idea of giving a housewife or a wife in 10 general a day off, especially if there are children. If there are little children involved, I think that is really great, and important.

Male Presenter: Of course.

Daniella Ramirez (Chile): Not only that, but for the husband to see how much the wife does in one day, especially with two kids, and she does that every day with no help, that is… 15

Male Presenter: So, you heard the husband say he will give his wife a day off every three months. What do you think about that?

Sarah: It should be (¹   ) (²   ) (³   ).

Humzah Goolam (Republic of South Africa): Yes.

Male Presenter: Petter? 20

Petter Weilenmann Higashi (Sweden): At least every month, every week.

Humzah: I think every weekend, at least on Saturdays and Sundays the wife should have a good time. She should be off.

Daniella: But it is a good start. I mean, they have promised, and it is a good beginning.

Male Presenter: It is (⁴   ) (⁵   ) (⁶   ). 25

Female Presenter: That is a good start.

Male Presenter: If you were to leave your housework, like in that family, what would happen?

Haliun Hatanbaatar (Mongolia): I also asked my husband to cook today, and he did, and then I had his cooking, and that was very good.

Male Presenter: So, it is natural. 30

Michael Thanner (Germany): My wife sometimes travels to visit her relatives outside of Tokyo, so I take care of the household, and my daughter. I mean, I get clear instructions from my wife, which helps, you know. She explains to me how the washing machine works.

Male Presenter: That is a good idea. Angela?

Angela: So even though there are just two people in my house, if I took the day off, I think it 35 would start to look like a single man's house. There would be laundry everywhere because my husband works out twice a day. So, there's dirty, stinky laundry everywhere, there would be dishes in the sink, the trash would be — and the cats wouldn't be fed. Like, there would be so much that needs to be done, I think.

Female Presenter: In one day? 40

Male Presenter: Xue, what about your house?

Shi Xue (China): If I go out for one day, there's going to be a party at home. So, you go back home, you find toys everywhere in the living room, basically they don't clean the room and they go out to eat, yes. And you are going to find your kid didn't do any homework at all.

Female Presenter: So just play. 45

Xue: Yes, it's going to be a father-son party.

Male Presenter: I see. Daniella, how about you?

Daniella: He would do most of the things that he has to do, like cooking, and cleaning, and things like that, but the house maybe will not be as organized. He doesn't like drying and folding the (7   )after drying them, so the clothes would be washed, dried, but still in the basket, 50 and they get so many wrinkles.

Male Narrator: Even though they said housework was shared 50/50, it seems the husbands are not all that good at it. So how do they manage?

Angela: I think part of it is also helping, like, let's do this together, a code word for "You did it wrong." So, let's do it together and now you know, so… 55

Daniella: Yes, otherwise they get unmotivated, and they take time to do it, and then you say something negative, I mean, they are not going to ever do it again. So, you have to think about that.

125

Angela: Together makes it better, I think.

Humzah: I just think women should teach them. 60

Male Presenter: Then, Humzah, you fold your clothes (8   )?

Humzah: Yes, I fold my clothes, like how my mom used to teach me, my grandmother used to teach me. Women should teach men how to do housework.

Male Presenter: Can you fold the clothes tidily?

Humzah: Okay, look, I mean, I wouldn't be able — because my hands are very muscular, so I am 65 not that delicate, you know. Women have an advantage. No, they have an advantage and they can do it better than men.

Angela: So, the answer is no.

Sarah: Well done, Humzah.

Daniella: You need to compliment. You need to tell them "Good job!" 70

Sarah: You should recognize that someone has done work for everyone, right?

Angela: You should definitely say "(9   ) (10   )," and, you know, give praise.

Male Presenter: Who does that?

Sarah: Of course.

Male Presenter: You do? 75

Sarah: No, it is just common (^{11}).

Angela: Yes, of course, it is just like…

Sarah: He should say "Thank you," and if he does, I say "Thank you."

Angela: Yes, I think so. He is (^{12}) to do it. He is just (^{13}) (^{14}) good at it. That is the difference. He is (^{15}) helpful, but he just sometimes doesn't always do it correctly. 80

Unit 7 Seafood

Risa Stegmayer (Female Presenter): Fotis, you went (¹   ) (²   ) Japanese seafood. What did you find to be coolest?

Fotis Vlachos (Greece): Other than the vast variety that I saw in the Japanese supermarkets, the way it's packed, presented in general, and the way they clean the fish, take the guts out, the bowels, and have it ready for instant consumption is amazing. I don't think we would ever see   5 something like this in Greece, and you know, it's just cool.

Shoji Kokami (Male Presenter): Oh, thank you. You don't see that in Greece? So, all of you, what do you think about the way fish are sold in Japanese supermarkets. Is it cool, or not cool?

Anis Boudraa (Algeria): Very cool.

Male Presenter: Cool? Really? Wow.   10

Mizhelle Agcaoili (Philippines): Because you have it sliced already, and prepared neatly, whereas in the Philippines you have to go to markets, and sometimes the fish are still jumping, and I'm quite afraid of that, actually.

Male Presenter: Ah. But that proves that they're (³   ).

Mizhelle: Some of them, yes. They're not cut like that.   15

Male Presenter: How are they sold in your countries, then? Not like this?

Anis: This way? No, no. You never find them…

Luz Gonzalez (Mexico): Well in Mexico, you can buy the fish whole or in pieces. It depends on   **127** your taste. But here in Japan, the fact that it's already done for you, it makes it easier to cook.

Male Presenter: Hmm, I see.   20

Ginny McKnight (Australia): Ours are (⁴   ) (⁵   ), I think. No bones, already (⁶   ) in some kind of breadcrumbs — ready for fish and chips. And mostly white fish — no heads, no tails, no bones. Straight in the pan, so…

Female Presenter: It no longer looks like a fish?

Ginny: In a kind of square. So, every fish…maybe it's whiting, or something like that…   25

Male Presenter: Square? Then, all you can make with it is fish and chips?

Ginny: True. We would go to like, maybe a (⁷   ) to eat other fish, but to cook at home, fish and chips is the (⁸   ) thing.

Male Presenter: I see. Norway is a seabound country…

Cato Stromsvik (Norway): Norway is surrounded by sea, and we have a lot of fish shops and stuff   30 like that. But I would say, maybe, the (⁹   ) of people they buy, like, the same as in Australia: frozen fish blocks. And it's really crazy, I was just reading about it actually, and they send frozen Norwegian-fished cod to China where they make it into fillets, and then they send it back to Europe. And this is a massive (¹⁰   ), and it covers all of Europe, basically.

Female Presenter: So, it goes and comes back.   35

Male Presenter: Huh! Well then, in your countries, how do you cook fish? How do you eat fish?

Luz: In Mexico, you prepare a big frying pan, with a lot of oil and a lot of garlic. So, you put in the fresh fish, it's just clean inside, and you put it in whole, and you fry both sides. And it's very tasty, because it's crunchy.

Flavio Parisi (Italy): Usually we avoid cutting the fish before cooking it because it's difficult. So, we just clean it up. When it's large, it's like, clean inside, and we put inside maybe, like, rosemary, garlic, and olive oil, and put it in the oven. It's a Sunday treat. 40

Male Presenter: Huh. Then why do you think fish sold in Japan is so conveniently cut, (^{11}), and packaged?

Anis: The service quality in Japan. It's not the only field where you find this high service quality. 45
I mean, they make it easy for the customers, and also, we talked about this previously, like, for *sashimi*, the way you cut it maybe makes it taste (^{12}).

Male Presenter: Do you think all this processing is a bit too much? Flavio, you always say "Too much, too much!"

Flavio: No, no, no. 50

Male Presenter: Why not?

Anis: I wish they'd do this in my country.

Flavio: No, I think this is perfect. It's all about knowledge. I think that ultimately, Japanese owe their lives to fish because of the protein they provide. So, you know, I think this kind of knowledge gets modernized and things become so easy. Everybody knows about fish. And, you 55
know, for us, it's meat. We treat meat in the same way.

Male Presenter: I see.

Flavio: We have a lot of choice. But, in Japan, there's not so much choice regarding meat.

Male Presenter: You have a point. I see.

Mizhelle: I think it's because people are very busy. And, yeah, coming from someone who never 60
cooked until I came to Japan, it's very convenient.

Male Presenter: That's a good point. You're (^{13}) (^{14}) to wait for fish to cook (^{15}) in an oven.

Female Presenter: Or to prepare it on your own.

Male Presenter: Yes. 65

Unit 8   Voice Actors

Risa Stegmayer (Female Presenter): So Anis, what did you think about that (¹   ) voice acting job?

Anis Boudraa (Algeria): So, about the voice actor, right, I thought she was very impressive and very professional. It wasn't just like giving information. She was giving information and also the purpose of the application was talking, and I found it very interesting actually. I found it cool,   5 actually.

Shoji Kokami (Male Presenter): Oh, what did the rest of you think?

Angela Schnabel (U.S.): I loved it. I thought it was awesome. I am going to (²   ) it when I get home. It was very cool.

João Orui (Brazil): I'll try that too.   10

Angela: Yes.

João: Is there a *samurai* mode for...

Anis: Actually, yes, there are so many voices, and that *samurai* was so cool, like it turned left and turned right, and he was giving orders, he was very cool.

Sumana Sripitak (Thailand): Yes, that's the first time I've ever seen that kind of application. I   15 think normally, we just hear something boring, the same thing, you know, a monotone but this is really fun. I want to try it, too.

Male Presenter: That's true.

Ginny McKnight (Australia): I think it's okay if you're walking but driving, it's so distracting. The girl's voice is so sexy, like what if you got too caught up in (³   ) (⁴   ) her   20 and you accidentally crash into something?

Male Presenter: That could be a problem if you get too much into the (⁵   ).

Female Presenter: Yes.

Vincent Findakly (France): In France too, we have that kind of thing. Like GPS with a variety of voices, not so many as in Japan but yes, we have a sexy woman's voice or we have a very famous   25 actor's voice.

Male Presenter: So, you do have things like that?

Anis: That's very dangerous.

Male Presenter: What sort of voices were you surprised to hear in Japan?

João: I think it was for (⁶   ) (⁷   ), where the bathroom actually is.   30

João: Like women's toilet to the right, men's to the left, like that.

Male Presenter: Okay.

Anis: I was pleasantly surprised by the ATM voice. So, she gives a lot of instructions and here in Japan, it gives instruction and...

Male Presenter: In English?   35

Anis: Yes, in English and in Japanese as well.

Petter Weilenmann Higashi (Sweden): It's so loud though, everything is so loud.

Anis: It's very loud, yes.

Petter: They don't need to know that I'm taking money out or that I am checking my balance and like… 40

Anis: That's true, yes.

Male Presenter: It's too loud. In your countries, the ([8]   ) ([9]   ) used for vending machines, baths, shops and such, are the voices for those done by real actors?

Anis: No. Not at all, I have never seen that in Algeria.

Male Presenter: Oh, you don't have voices for those things at all? No voice announcing that the 45
bath is ready in your countries?

Anis: No.

Male Presenter: No? What about ATMs? Don't they have voices?

Anis: No voices in Algeria.

Male Presenter: No voices? No voices. 50

Anis: No.

Male Presenter: Is there too much talking in Japan, do you think? Is it too much or is it considerate?

João: I think there's a lot of talking in Japan, like even the bathroom is talking to you.

Anis: Actually, I used to think so too, like everything is talking here. You are assaulted all the time 55
by voices and noises. But once I went back home, I had that reverse culture shock, like "Why is
nothing talking here? Why is there no instruction? Why?" — so, when you get used to it, actually,
it's very convenient.

Male Presenter: Is voice guidance in Japan cool then or ([10]   ) ([11]   )?
Cool? Really? Really? 60

Angela: Yeah, It's polite.

Male Presenter: What?

Angela: Yes, it makes me feel good. It's polite.

Anis: It's polite, yes.

Male Presenter: Why? 65

Anis: Politeness is nice.

Angela: Yes, yes.

Petter: The vending machine saying "Thank you," is cool.

Angela: Yes.

Male Presenter: Okay. Well, as we said, these are not computer-generated voices, but real human 70
voices. So, what do you think about most of the voice guidance in Japan using the voices of real
human voice actors? How do you feel?

João: It is warm, I think. People like to hear people talking rather than robots.

Angela: It gives people a job, which I think is awesome.

Petter: Yes. 75

Angela: Yes.

Male Presenter: Would a car navigation system with the voices of voice actors be popular in your countries? It could become popular?

Anis: If adapted, it might. If they adapt the language, it might work because...

Male Presenter: Ginny?

80

Ginny: We would — if it was like Brad Pitt's voice or something, maybe a (^{12}) actor's voice, if it was like that, we would be into it.

Male Presenter: (^{13}) (^{14}) (^{15})?

Ji Yang (China): I don't think it would be popular in China, because we just don't care about the voice, what kind of voice.

85

Male Presenter: You don't care?

Yang: No.

Sumana: I think it would be really popular. Yes, especially if you do like, the anime voice in the navigation, like *Doraemon* or like...

Male Presenter: Oh, *Doraemon*.

90

Summana: It's really big in Thailand.

Male Presenter: I might buy that, too. "Keep going, keep going. I know there's traffic, but don't give up."

Anis: Because, with that application, she keeps talking and she changes the topic. And the more you use it, the more miles you travel. And then if she becomes friendlier and she changes the topic.

95

131

Male Presenter: Wow, that's great.

Vincent: What I like about Japan is just they are always thinking about making people's life funnier. So, yeah, I like it.

Risa Stegmayer (Female Presenter): So, Yang, how was your outing?

Ji Yang (China): Yeah, I heard some of the Japanese dumplings, fried dumplings, are very popular in China because they are sold in some of the *ramen* shops. So we discovered many kinds of very Japanese dumplings, like they put in *mentaiko*, they put in *shiso*. Those kinds of dumplings. I think they taste good. I like them.   5

Shoji Kokami (Male Presenter): So you can accept them as dumplings?

Yang: Not the *gyoza* as I know them. Yeah, a kind of Japanese dish.

Male Presenter: Do any of you have thoughts about this?

Yura Yefymenko (Russia): I love *gyoza*.

Pafan Julsaksrisakul (Thailand): In Thailand we are only familiar with Japanese ones. So, for me,   10
I'm not sure if, like, Japanese is better or not, but I like Japanese a lot.

Male Presenter: I see.

Omer Ishag (Sudan): The rice was added to the meal, though. I think the *gyoza* can
(¹   ) (²   ), without the rice or noodles.

Yang: The *ramen* and rice together. It's strange. Yeah.   15

Flavio Parisi (Italy): Exactly. Like you have *gyoza*. We have some kind of *gyoza*, or dumplings, in Italian food. It's called *ravioli* or *tortellini*. Basically, it's the same idea. But rice or pasta with pasta. So, you know, it's a matter of balance.

132

Male Presenter: We have a lot of opinions, but (³   ) (⁴   ) (⁵   ).
Oh, Omer, you have curry rice?   20

Omer: Yes, Japanese curry and rice is quite similar to foods in my country.

Male Presenter: Japanese curry rice is more like Sudanese (⁶   ) than Indian curry is?

Omer: Yes. Especially beef curry. Maybe not other curries, but beef curry is quite similar.

Male Presenter: How about the others? Who likes curry? Japanese curry? Oh! (⁷   )
(⁸   ). Flavio, you like curry? You like it?   25

Flavio: Yeah. That is a good style of the Japanized food, I think. I used to live in India, also, so I love Indian food. So, you know, this is something completely different, original, and special and…yeah, it's OK.

Male Presenter: It's the same with *Napolitan*.

Female Presenter: Right, right.   30

Male Presenter: The same as *Napolitan*…

Flavio: No, I'm not buying it.

Male Presenter: Kelly has a hamburger steak. Is that cool? Is hamburger steak a Japanized dish?

Kelly Riley (U.S.): Yeah, in America, you're not gonna just get a hamburger patty. if you're gonna get it, it's gonna be a hamburger. (⁹   ) (¹⁰   ) (¹¹   )   35
(¹²   ) that we have to it is, like, meatloaf, but it's (¹³   ) different, though.

Male Presenter: This is a (¹⁴   ). You don't have it in the U.S.?

Kelly: No, not at all.

Male Presenter: No. In the U.S.?

Kelly: Hamburger. 40

Female Presenter: Steak? Not hamburger steak?

Kelly: No. Not that I'm aware of. I've never… yeah, it wasn't until I came to Japan, and I didn't really…

Male Presenter: Have you ever been surprised to find dishes in Japan that are localized (^{15}) of dishes from your countries?   45

Yang: *Chuka-don* and *tenshin-don*, which have a Chinese name. But I never see it in China.

Male Presenter: We won't find *tenshin-don* in Tianjin?

Yang: No, no, we don't have that in Tianjin.

Male Presenter: Huh? Have you ever tried *chuka-don* or *tenshin-don*?

Yang: Yes.   50

Male Presenter: How were they?

Yang: I like them.

Pafan: I found this very weird, like, coriander *ramen*. You know, here it is called *pakuchi*.

Male Presenter: Oh.

Pafan: That type of, like, vegetable that you put in, like, very smelly, very pungent. Yeah, but   55 they make it a *ramen*, which I find very weird. We never have that.

133

Shoji Kokami (Male Presenter): Recently, tablet computers have gotten bigger — you know what I mean. What do you do with those? You can't put them in your pocket.

Craig Taylor (Australia): Hang on. I'd go back a question: why do you want to carry that round with you anyway? You know, what's the point? It's gonna stay in your bag all day, so why not just leave it (^{1}) (^{2})?   5

Nicolas Seraphin (France): I think, maybe, it also comes from the fact that, in Japan, you're always expected to have everything on you, like, to be ready to face any kind of situation. So, you have to have tissues, you have to have, you know, like, basically everything so that you can go, "OK, here you go," or "I'm ready for any kind of situation," and that makes a big difference. So even for men, that's why we have bags.   10

Male Presenter: Interesting.

Heike Brock (Germany): For German men it's more like, I think, they are just too practical. They don't want to carry anything around, they want to have their hands free, to do whatever they want, and they are like, yeah, so just put it in their pocket and leave. It's more like a practical thing.   15

Male Presenter: I see.

Raffaele Lima (Brazil): Actually, I think it's the type of bag. OK. If it's a backpack, it's fine — it's very masculine. But, like, we saw in the video, like, the guy with the leather bag. That one is too fashionable for a man.

Ryan Gaines (U.S.): No, don't say… We're all human, OK? We're all human — you can have   20 a bag if you're a man. I learned that. Really — it's OK. It's OK, really. I think all these guys here, we're (^{3}) of having bags, because people will think we're (^{4}), or something. (^{5}) (^{6}) (^{7}) — it's a bag.

Female Presenter: Another question was why Japanese women carry their bags like this, on their arms. Was this question answered?   25

Raffaele: No, I couldn't. It's sort of, inside myself, I still think this is a very Japanese way of carrying a bag. It's too, like…if you want to imitate a Japanese lady, I think that would be one gesture.

Male Presenter: Oh.

Heike: Actually, now I'm in Japan, I do it. I started doing it when I came here. I was like "What   30 is that?" But now I'm doing it because it's (^{8}) (^{9}) (^{10}), for example, when I go through the (^{11}) (^{12}). I have my ticket, so I can hold the bag and touch at the same time. But in Germany you don't do it.

Male Presenter: I see. OK. Do women carry bags like that in other countries? Oh, they do?

Ryan: In America.   35

Male Presenter: In America?

Ryan: American women do that.

Male Presenter: Really?

Ryan: This is more common, but girls do this, too.

Male Presenter: What type of woman? 40

Ryan: Like, the ladylike…

Male Presenter: The elegant ones! Elegant ladies.

Ryan: Like, they want to look very…

Male Presenter: They do this to look ladylike — is that what you're saying?

Ryan: Yes. 45

Male Presenter: Genteel? Ladylike?

Ryan: Yes.

Male Presenter: Oh, is that so? Same in France?

Nicolas: Yeah, yeah, yeah.

Male Presenter: I see. So, it makes them look feminine. 50

Craig: In Australia, if we do that, we are mocking an old lady. Yeah, yeah, "Yes, you know, I'm an old lady," 'cos they carry their bags like that in Australia.

Male Presenter: I see.

Raffaele: But my first impression, in Japan, ladies look much older when they carry a bag like that. 55

Male Presenter: OK.

Male Narrator: Next, let's look at "bags in bags," which are (^{13}) among women these days.

Female Presenter: It has (^{14}) (^{15}) pockets, like for your seal, your pen, and your keys. If you have one of these, you don't forget things, so it's convenient. 60

Male Presenter: What do you think about that?

Raffaele: That's very cool, very cool, very convenient.

Linh Tran (Vietnam): Because, like, it's simple, if I have a big bag, I put many things in it. So when I want to look for something, it's like "Where is it, where is it?" something like that. So, I think this is much more convenient. 65

Male Presenter: You think so? How about you, Heike?

Heike: I think it's practical, but probably I wouldn't use it myself. When I go out, I always count to have everything, so I know I need…7, 8 items that I need to have in my bag. And I always count them, and then I am "OK, 7 or 8 are there," so I go out. And so I don't really need the extra bag. 70

Male Presenter: Oh, I see. Raffaele?

Raffaele: I really like it. In a society like Japan, you need things fast, like "OK, this is my card, I need to go and do things faster." So if you have these organized, it's very convenient.

Male Presenter: All right.

Shoji Kokami (Male Presenter): You know, once this show is aired overseas, a mass of people will come here.

Risa Stegmayer (Female Presenter): I'm sure. So, Haliun, you made the visit. What did you think of the health screening in Japan?

Haliun Hatanbaatar (Mongolia): I'm pretty surprised that, Japanese senior citizens, are very self- 5
conscious and self-aware. They are highly aware of their health. So, basically, it's not really a cheap thing, but it's a kind of investment in one's own health. Yeah, so it's pretty good. Yeah.

Male Presenter: I see. Are comprehensive health screenings like this available in your countries?

Collectively: No.

Male Presenter: No? No! Oh no? Really? Not even the U.S.? 10

Zak Elliot (U.S.): I wouldn't say no, but it wouldn't be very common to go and get these
(^{1}).

Male Presenter: Then in your countries, how do people detect diseases at the early stages?

Ginny McKnight (Australia): She said that when you reach a certain age, you sometimes get a letter from the (^{2}) or from the healthcare provider. So, they will send you a letter, 15
saying like "Oh you're 65, you might have, like, breast cancer or something, so please take this letter to the doctor and then you can get it (^{3}) (^{4})."

Male Presenter: Oh, it's free?

Ginny: But it's usually not...unless you request it, it's not an all-over scan, it's more for just common diseases or common cancers... 20

Male Presenter: I see.

Ginny: It's a little different.

Zak: In America, maybe the feeling is more that it's not so much, like, the exact (^{5})
(^{6}) etc. that'll tell you if you're healthy or not, but you should be (^{7}) of your body and of any changes... 25

Male Presenter: Oh really?

Flavio Parisi (Italy): In Italy it's the same. You always have a relationship with the family doctor, so, like, usually if you have some symptoms, then he will prescribe you, like, a check, at the hospital. It will be helped by machines eventually.

Male Presenter: In Japan, employers arrange annual health checkups, even for young people. 30
But how is it in your countries? Anyone have these? Oh, in the Philippines. Oh. Mongolia, too? France also? Zak...no?

Zak: No, because...it felt a bit strange to me that, coming to Japan, that our HR department would know what my health results are. That's my personal information, right?

Female Presenter: Oh yeah. 35

Male Presenter: I see.

Female Presenter: It's personal.

Male Presenter: That's a good point. OK. OK, I'll change the question now. The number of people in Japan taking periodic health screenings has increased by 70% in the last nine years. Why do you think that is? Why are 70% more people taking the screenings in Japan? 40

Flavio: The more people go, the more you hear "Oh, he went there!" So, it's just, you know, about knowing, so it's just exponential, I think, you know. Like some people around you went so, "Oh, let's go."

Male Presenter: That's (⁸   ) true.

Haliun: I also think that Japanese people, they don't like this kind of excuse. Like "Oh, I feel   45 fine." So, unless, you know, like, for example, in my country, if people feel, like, some pain, they will go to the hospital. Even if they are fine, they still go for the checkup. So, this is a very big difference.

Male Presenter: Mmm. Ginny?

Ginny: I also noticed on normal Japanese television, how often they have medical shows on   50 (⁹   ) (¹⁰   ). So sometimes, some famous comedians will say "That comedian can do it, maybe I can do it too." So...

Male Presenter: OK. Professor, what do you say?

Professor: Yes, well, as for the physical checkups and comprehensive health screenings in Japan, one factor is our governmental policy that makes us form the (¹¹   ) of having   55 checkups at certain points in our (¹²   ), such as 1-year-old checkups and also pre-school checkups. Another factor is that our (¹³   ) organizations, from a personnel management standpoint, (¹⁴   ) their employees to have checkups, in order to minimize sick leave and epidemics. Those factors have led to our habit, our natural inclination to take physical checkups periodically. And for early detection and early treatment of diseases, we tend   60 to opt for the comprehensive health screening courses. By taking these courses once a year, we feel we are preventing diseases from becoming (¹⁵   ) and making it difficult for us to continue our jobs or our social activities. I think those are the thoughts behind this trend.

Male Presenter: I see.

137

Risa Stegmayer (Female Presenter): Right. So, Anna, what do you have to say about your visit?

Anna Schrade (Germany): It was really impressive because I use Japanese coins every day, but I have never really had the time to look at them closely and I never expected something like this. So, it is amazing how beautiful they are and what thought is behind them too.

Shoji Kokami (Male Presenter): All right. What do you think about these minting technologies? 5 What do you think, Craig? Cool?

Craig Taylor (Australia): Yes, the same. The (¹   ), the (²   ), and how you can find that the 500 yen written-- I have never seen that before.

Magnus Devold (Norway): It was amazing, yes. Japan is unique in making coins this advanced.

Male Presenter: Okay. Who else? 10

David Pavlina (U.S.): What I like is that the anti-counterfeiting measures are also very artistic. I think other countries may not (³   ) (⁴   ) so much to the artistic value of the anti-counterfeiting measures, but I think Japan blends the two together. It is an anti-counterfeiting measure, but it is very beautiful at the same time.

Male Presenter: I see. Does anyone else think Japanese money designs are beautiful? Who says 15 yes? Really? This is surprising. You are not just being nice, are you? Are you being honest?

Nicolas Seraphin (France): As I said before, but actually in our country, the money tends to look more and more like, you know, Monopoly currency, like the game. Whereas this looks very, I would say, trustworthy, like very real money, old-fashioned, that is what I like about it.

Marilia Melo (Brazil): One thing I love about the coins, especially compared to American dollars, 20 that they have the numbers on them. On U.S. dollars, they don't have numbers. You need to read how much —each of them is worth. It is very very hard.

Female Presenter: They read (⁵   ) (⁶   ) in letters instead of numerals.

Marilia: They don't have any numbers, they only have letters.

Magnus: I think, yes, the scenery, the nature, they really captured all the Japanese beauty into a 25 small piece of paper.

Male Presenter: I see.

Male Narrator: Do money designs reflect national characteristics? We asked the participants to show their money.

Jackie Mwangi (Kenya): In my country, we use presidents. So, both the paper money and the 30 coins, and it doesn't matter if it was a good president or bad president, he is on the money.

Male Presenter: Yes, I see.

Jackie: But what I really think especially about the Japanese paper money is the fact that you use people who have achieved much. Like, for instance, you have Hideyo Noguchi, you have Ichiyo Higuchi. 35

Male Presenter: Right. Okay. Who are those on your Norwegian bills?

Magnus: This is an opera singer, and this is a writer. I think so, yes.

Female Presenter: They are women.

Male Presenter: Interesting. So that opera singers are (^{7}) (^{8})?

Magnus: I only heard of her because of the hundred krone bill actually. But now they are changing the (^{9}).   40

Male Narrator: These are the new Norwegian bills that are due for issue in (^{10}). The front sides have marine themes. There are patterns on the back. They are drawing high attention as being innovative.

Male Presenter: Is everyone in Norway (^{11}) about the designs changing from   45
notable figures to patterns?

Magnus: I don't know. I like it to be more classic like this or even better, the yen.

Male Presenter: Okay, what else other than politicians?

Marilia: In Brazil, they actually have animals and nature like this.

Male Presenter: No humans?   50

Marilia: No. on the other side there is a face, but this is not someone specifically, it is just a face.

Male Presenter: I see. All the others have politicians. The Chinese bills have politicians, Mao Zedong, and that is Lincoln.

David: Most of our currency has presidents' faces. And in fact, the U.S. is currently redesigning the bills to have more without presidents, in fact. They are looking at people like Martin Luther   55
King Jr. and other famous (^{12}) instead of using, …right.

Male Presenter: Oh, really? Professor?

Professor: Yes, Japanese money depicts nature, but it's mostly (^{13}) and that's a very
interesting fact, actually. Take the rice stalks for example. The 500-yen coin is similar. Perhaps
it's all about the blessings of nature. Rice is symbolic of Japan. There are also images of Mt. Fuji.   60
All are beauties of nature. Our money depicts what we consider beautiful in nature. Money is
something backed up by (^{14}) (^{15}), so it seems more natural to depict
political figures, but this is not done in Japan, and it's quite unique. I think the way Japanese
regard money is hidden somewhere in this.

Male Presenter: Interesting.   65

139

Risa Stegmayer (Female Presenter): What did you discover hunting for Japanese monkeys? Peter?

Peter Macy (U.S.): Ah, you know, for me, I thought, I mean, this was something really interesting, this monkey mountain. And I learned that they call them *o-saru*, with the "o" in front, to make it, like, polite. You know, in my country, we like bears and dogs and cats; monkeys aren't so popular. 5
But I was really surprised that (^{1}) (^{2}) (^{3}) kept checking out this monkey mountain.

Shoji Kokami (Male Presenter): Well, it's true. We don't say *o-zou san* when we speak of (^{4}), or *o-kirin san* when we talk of giraffes. Japanese people probably also find that interesting. 10

Female Presenter: A new (^{5}).

Male Presenter: In your countries, is it the same? Are monkeys popular in your countries? And what do you think about the popularity of monkeys here?

Dimitris Kontopoulos (Greece): Well, in Greece we don't have any monkeys because the climate is a little bit different, so monkeys don't live in Greece. So, I guess Greek people don't like 15
or dislike monkeys. We just think of them as exotic animals. Somewhere far away, not really connected to us.

Male Presenter: I see.

Nicolas Seraphin (France): I think French people wouldn't be so overjoyed by seeing monkeys. And the "o", as we just mentioned, the "o" of *o-saru san* is actually very interesting. Yeah. 20

Male Presenter: Hmmm. China's different, right?

Shi Xue (China): Of course. Well, monkeys are popular in China. There are lots of monkeys. And, they are one of our favorite animals. So, you can always find monkeys in our stories, like, we have this famous novel…

Male Presenter: (^{6}) to the West! 25

Xue: *Saiyuki*! So, we feel very close, we feel very connected…

Male Presenter: I see. When you hear the word "monkey", do you have a positive or negative impression? What image of monkeys do you have in your countries, would you say?

Nathalie Lobue (Switzerland): Tricky.

Male Presenter: Tricky? 30

Collectively: Yeah. Sneaky.

Yenny Sotomayor (Peru): Because they're always, like, trying to steal food and, yeah, and…

Male Presenter: That's negative.

Yenny: Yeah , yeah, it's negative…

Nicolas: In France we have an expression which is, "monkey money", and monkey money 35
means, like, fake money, basically.

Male Presenter: Wow.

Nicolas: I think that's pretty witty, not in a good way but…

Female Presenter: They're cunning.

Male Presenter: Hmm. 40

Willy Yanthy (Indonesia): Of course monkeys are smart, but when someone is upset, they can say "you are monkey," and it's not a good meaning, actually.

Male Presenter: Hmmm. Well, who has a positive impression? Oh, there are places with a positive impression! I see.

Xue: And in China people actually choose which year they would like to have their children. 45 They would prefer a monkey year, because that's positive, because we have a positive image for monkeys.

Female Presenter: Not the dragon?

Xue: Dragon, of course, that's another very good…

Male Presenter: OK. I (^{7}) (^{8}). 50

Xue: I think that really depends on people but really dragons, monkeys, horses, are very good images.

Male Presenter: Oh, amazing!

Female Presenter: In Japan, the word "monkey" generally (^{9}) (^{10}) primates. Other than humans, here we introduce some representative (^{11}). 55

Male Narrator: Chimpanzees and gorillas live in Africa. Orangutans, gibbons etc. are found in Asia. There are many other kinds of monkeys. But most of their habitats are in the tropics and subtropics, such as Africa, Asia, and South and Central America.

141

Female Presenter: There are no monkeys in Europe and North America.

Male Presenter: Oh. 60

Female Presenter: Mmm, interesting fact.

Male Presenter: Wow, there are no monkeys in Europe and North America.

Female Presenter: Right.

Peter: My image of monkeys is very loud and kind of playful. All the Japanese monkeys stand like Japanese people. They look like they're (^{12}) (^{13}) (^{14}) 65 (^{15}).

Female Presenter: Next, what aspect did you think was cool, Yenny?

Yenny: OK, so this one is when we went to the temple and we found this statue. I think this is important because we can see the mother with a little baby. So, a lot of families were there to pray for fertility. Also, they were asking for a child, for a healthy one. So, I think it's pretty cool 70 to have this in Japan.

Male Presenter: I see. It seems that monkeys are pretty popular in Japan.

Expert: Adding an "o" appears to be used for important things inside the house, for example chopsticks — *o-hashi* and money — *o-kane*. So, we add an "o" to special things inside the house, but not to things outside the house. When you see the old picture scrolls, you can see horse 75 stables in royal palaces, and next to them are monkeys. That means that monkeys are servants of the gods that protect horses. So, you have to have monkeys next to the horse stables. This means that monkeys and horses aren't kept outdoors but are considered indoor animals. And why are monkeys with horses? Well, monkeys drive away threatening disasters and evil spirits. There's a theory that this is because the word for monkey also means "to leave," so it's a play on words. The monkeys are able to prevent bad things from happening or to prevent harm from coming to the horses also.

Web動画のご案内 **StreamLine**

本テキストの映像は、オンラインでのストリーミング再生になります。下記URLよりご利用ください。なお**有効期限は、はじめてログインした時点から1年半**です。

http://st.seibido.co.jp

①

ログイン画面

🔒 LOGIN

テキストに添付されているシールをはがして、12桁のアクセスコードをご入力ください。

[　　] - [　　] - [　　]

同意してログイン

以下の「利用規約」をご確認頂き、同意する場合は上記ボタン【同意してログイン】を押してください。

利用規約

1. このウェブサイト（以下「本サイト」といいます）は、株式会社成美堂（以下「弊社」といいます）が運営しています。弊社の商品・サービス（以下「本サービス」といいます）利用時の会員登録の有無を問わず、本サイトの利用にあたっては以下のご利用条件をお読み頂き、これらの条件にご同意の上ご利用ください。

2. 本サービスに関して個別に利用規約がある場合、本規約に加えそれらも適用されます。

3. 本サイトを通じて、弊社の商品を販売する第三者のウェブサイトにご案内ないしリンクされることがあります。リンク先ウェブサイトにおいて取得された個人情報は

> 巻末に添付されているシールをはがして、アクセスコードをご入力ください。

②

メニュー画面

AFP World Focus
—Environment, Health, and Technology—
アクセスコード有効期限: 2018年4月30日

🎬 **Video**　　🎵 **Audio**

Lesson 1: Global Warming and Climat... >
Lesson 2: Diet and Health for Long ... >
Lesson 3: Self-Driving for the Futu... >
Lesson 4: Sustaining Biodiversity a... >
Lesson 5: 3D Printers for Creating ... >
Lesson 6: IT and Education >
Lesson 7: Protection from Natural D... >
Lesson 8: Practical Uses of Drones ... >

> 「Video」または「Audio」を選択すると、それぞれストリーミング再生ができます。

③

再生画面

AFP World Focus
—Environment, Health, and Technology—
アクセスコード有効期限: 2018年4月30日

▶

Lesson 2:
Diet and Health for Long Lives
食習慣：長生きのためのスーパーフードを探す

> **推奨動作環境**
>
> 【PC OS】
> Windows 7~　/　Mac 10.8~
>
> 【Mobile OS】
> iOS　/　Android　※Android の場合は4.x~が推奨
>
> 【Desktop ブラウザ】
> Internet Explorer 9~ / Firefox / Chrome / Safari

TEXT PRODUCTION STAFF

edited by	編集
Eiichi Tamura	田村 栄一
Yasutaka Sano	佐野 泰孝

cover design by	表紙デザイン
sein	ザイン

text design by	本文デザイン
sein	ザイン

CD PRODUCTION STAFF

narrated by	吹き込み者
Howard Colefield (AmE)	ハワード・コールフィールド（アメリカ英語）
Karen Haedrich (AmE)	カレン・ヘドリック（アメリカ英語）
Dominic Allen (AmE)	ドミニク・アレン（アメリカ英語）
Ilana Labourene (AmE)	イラーナ・ラボリン（アメリカ英語）

Discovering Cool Japan
発掘! かっこいいニッポンー異文化理解から日本文化発信へー

2019年1月10日 初 版 発 行
2022年3月5日 第4刷 発 行

著　者　津田 晶子
　　　　金志 佳代子
　　　　Christopher Valvona

発行者　佐野 英一郎
発行所　株式会社 成美堂
　　　　〒101-0052　東京都千代田区神田小川町3-22
　　　　TEL 03-3291-2261　FAX 03-3293-5490
　　　　https://www.seibido.co.jp

印刷・製本　三美印刷（株）

ISBN 978-4-7919-7187-9　　　　　　　　　　Printed in Japan

Map of Japan

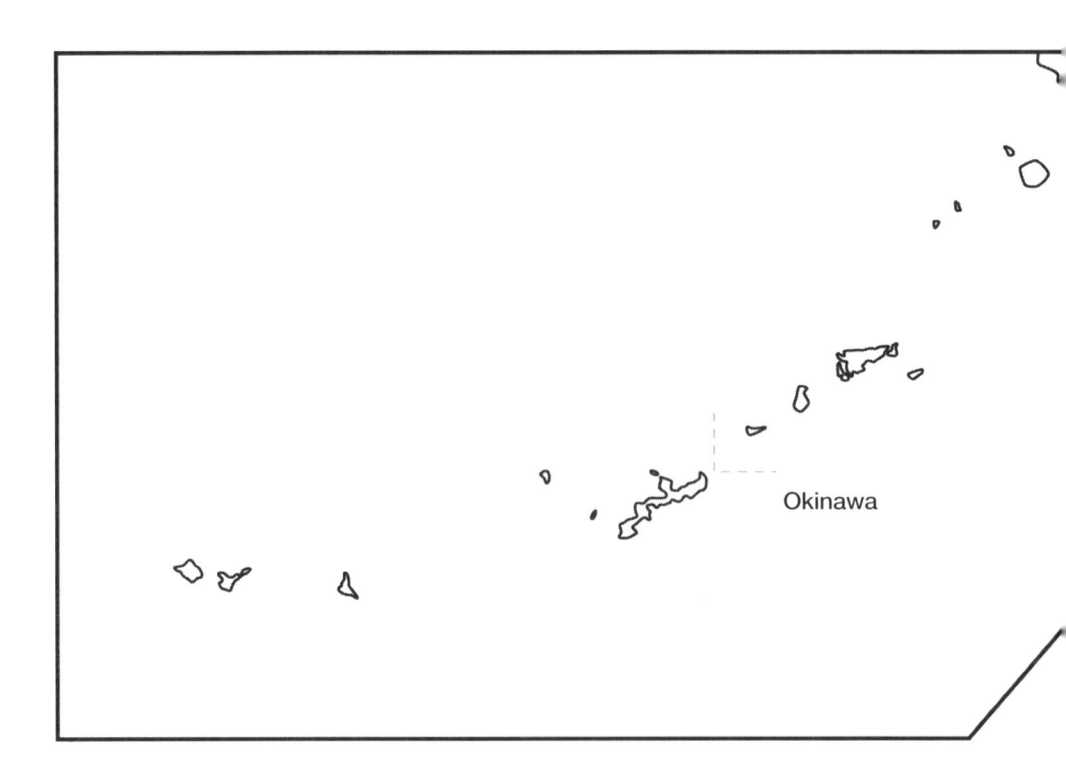